A Snowflake in My Hand

SAMANTHA MOONEY

CORGI BOOKS

TRANSWORLD PUBLISHERS
61-63 Uxbridge Road, London W5 5SA
A Random House Company
www.transworldbooks.co.uk

A SNOWFLAKE IN MY HAND
A CORGI BOOK: 9780552167796

First published in Great Britain
in 1990 by Bantam Books
an imprint of Transworld Publishers
Reissued as a Corgi paperback edition 2013

The book is a work of non-fiction based on the life,
experiences and recollections of the author.

Addresses for Random House Limited companies outside the UK
can be found at: www.randomhouse.co.uk
The Random House Group Ltd Reg. No. 954009.

The Random House Group Limited supports the Forest Stewardship
Council® (FSC®), the leading international forest-certification organisation.
Our books carrying the FSC label are printed on FSC®-certified paper. FSC
is the only forest-certification scheme supported by the leading environmental
organisations, including Greenpeace. Our paper procurement policy can be
found at www.randomhouse.co.uk/environment

2 4 6 8 10 9 7 5 3 1

Printed and bound by CPI Group (UK) Ltd, Croydon, CR0 4YY

MIX
Paper from
responsible sources
FSC® C016897
www.fsc.org

I would like to thank Nick Lyons, who guided and encouraged me at every step. His support was unfaltering from the beginning.

I thank Eleanor Friede, Barbara Bowen, and Jeanne Bernkopf for their special care, attention, and expertise. . . .

I extend my gratitude to the clients and patients at our clinic who have allowed me to share a few moments in their lives.

My footsteps mount the slight incline, the first to pass this way. The snow falls gently, muffling New York City's shrieking sounds. My mind, unfocused, follows up the hill and on to Maine. Wooded, solitary chambers of silence broken only by the crunching of snow packed underfoot.

Then I see him, and he summons all my senses and awakens me, as he always does, to the reality about him. The black cat poses on the windowsill, grooming his glossy coat as if to punctuate his contrast with the snow. The domesticated panther, he sits in his jungle of houseplants and shares the sun with them. But it is his ledge, and he has inched the plants precariously edgeward to accommodate his lengthy well-being. I smile to think of the plants that have been swept off the carpet and repotted, and wonder if the new window display is his.

I do not know his people, but in the years that I have marked my progress by his presence in the window, I have felt a fondness for those who love him. Strangers they remain, these folk who feed and fawn over their sassy cat, but I have singled out their brownstone, this brownstone, mirrored by brownstones. This is where the black cat lives.

Chapter 1

My alarm clock failed to ring, but by skipping morning coffee I managed to be only fifteen minutes late. As the elevator crawled to the eighth floor of the Animal Medical Center I hoped that perhaps Clancy too had overslept. It was 7:20. The elevator door opened, and I stepped into the hall to find him waiting.

"I know I'm late, Clancy, but it happens occasionally." He looked angry. "If you would just wait until I come get you, you wouldn't have to pace in the corridor."

I unlocked the office door, and he brushed past me as he entered. I opened the drawer immediately, knowing there would be no peace until he got what he wanted. Clancy was not a finicky eater and promptly concentrated on his breakfast.

He was a square-jawed, tiger-suited cat, seven years old.

Short-legged and sturdy, he looked like a prize fighter who had retired from the ring.

When I was on time, I would find him in his cage in the ward if the wardman had remembered to close the cage door securely. The door had to be lifted slightly for the lock to click. As soon as I opened the cage Clancy would meow, hug me, and then crawl over my shoulder and jump to the floor. Before I did the morning treatments, I would open the ward door so that he could run to the office where the food was waiting. But if I was even five minutes late, he would meet me at the elevator, as he had today, and reprimand me. I never knew how he got out the ward door.

Dr. Hayes came into the office. Audrey had completed her residency at the Animal Medical Center with a specialty in oncology, the study of masses or tumors. She was now an associate staff member. We had first worked together on Saturday night medical clinics. We both liked working with cats, and we both were unconventional in our restraint techniques: we tried to pay attention to the cat's preferences.

Dr. Hayes patted Clancy on the head. He glared at her.

"You know, Samantha, Clancy's using you. He's a male chauvinist, just like T.C." T.C. was one of her six cats.

"That may be true, Audrey, but Clancy and I have an understanding." Clancy yawned and walked away, confident that I would defend him.

"He's rude, arrogant, and ungrateful."

"He's handsome and Irish."

I heard Greg's voice in the corridor outside the office. Dr. MacEwen was the head of the unit.

"In the parking lot? It must have come from the stables across the street. Will it be all right in this box? What about food?"

"I put some water in there and some bread," the clinic aide replied. "I'm just afraid to leave it downstairs in the clinic, in case someone knocks it over. It's quieter up here, if you don't mind, and I'll take it home this afternoon."

"Morning, Audrey, Sam." Greg was carrying a shoe box with tiny holes punched in the top. "One of the aides found this mouse, and I told her we'd keep it out of the way for her this morning. What's Clancy doing out?" We all turned and looked at Clancy now sleeping soundly on the counter, snuggled in a corner. I thought I saw his ear twitch, but he did not move.

"He's exhausted, Greg."

"He never does anything. Put him back in his cage."

"But he's sick."

"He's not sick. Granted, he has the feline leukemia virus, but it doesn't faze him in the least."

"But he was abandoned. He thinks no one loves him."

Greg was weakening, as he always did with Clancy. Looking at the shoe box, he said, "What about the—"

"Clancy's too tired even to notice. You know he can't sleep when he's in his cage."

"Poor Clancy," Greg replied, smiling as he left the office.

Clancy stretched and shifted his position.

I had first met Clancy a few months after I started working in Oncology. We see most of our cancer patients on the eighth floor, but I was still working Tuesday and Saturday nights with Greg and Audrey in the general clinic on the second floor, where medical and surgical cases, routine examinations, vaccinations, and emergencies are handled.

When I walked into the exam booth that Tuesday night, Clancy was sitting on the metal table. I usually have to pry my cats out of their carrier when they visit the doctor, so I was

5

impressed by his nonchalance. He stared at me defiantly and then began to groom himself. When Greg came in, Clancy lay on his side and stared wistfully into space.

Clancy's owner had three cats. The other two had tested negative for the feline leukemia virus. Because the virus is contagious among cats, Clancy's mistress had brought Clancy to be euthanized. He was her husband's cat; she had brought him in because her husband could not bear to.

Leukemia is an abnormal proliferation of white blood cells in the bloodstream and bone marrow. In cats most leukemias are caused by the leukemia virus, but not all cats with the virus develop leukemia.

The virus, found in a small percentage of cats in the general population, can be passed from cat to cat in the saliva, urine, milk, and blood. In other words, a communal litter pan and feeding dishes are likely intermediaries for the virus, as are a bite wound, or a mother cat nursing her kittens. Not all cats exposed to the virus will become viremic, or persistently infected. Some cats develop antibodies against the virus within three months of exposure to a positive cat, and therefore become immune to the infection.

We had been able to send a magnificent long-haired cat home to his grateful owner after the cat rejected the leukemia virus on his own. We didn't see a case like this often, but such things did happen.

We do not know which cats will become viremic and which immune, but we believe that kittens and older or debilitated cats are more susceptible because their immune systems are either not fully developed or are altered. In any event it takes more than one test to confirm that a cat has the virus.

A cat who tests positive for the leukemia virus may be a healthy pet with a glossy coat, good appetite, and normal activity. I remember a feisty calico cat with eyes the colors of stained glass who probably became positive late in her life. She lived to the age of twenty-one.

I had long been fascinated by this virus that remains dormant in some cats and causes fatal diseases in others. It was generally believed that the positive cats were more susceptible to disease because their immune systems, the body's defense, were suppressed by the leukemia virus. I had asked Greg if we could use on Clancy a new form of therapy that we had been testing—therapy meant to stimulate Clancy's immune system so that, ideally, he would reject the virus, or at least resist the diseases associated with the virus. Greg had agreed, and we had suggested this treatment to Clancy's mistress as an alternative to euthanasia.

When I lifted Clancy from the table, he had rested both front paws on either side of my neck. As we headed for the elevator to take us to the eighth floor, his new home, I heard Greg's voice. "Just this one, Sam. And remember, don't get too attached." But Clancy was purring.

Greg set the ground rules for Clancy's stay with us. Clancy must remain in a cage. He must not interfere with the Oncology Unit's routine. I appealed to Greg's sense of fairness. After all, Clancy was a pet, unaccustomed to prolonged confinement. Greg gave Clancy his first inch, and Clancy slowly and relentlessly stretched it until the entire eighth floor was his.

Clancy was allowed in the office before clinic for breakfast. Duerrel, our wardman, usually cleaned the ward between 7 and 9 A.M., and then Clancy could return to a clean cage. A few mornings clinic started early, and by the time his cage was ready I was busy with patients. Clancy wisely camouflaged himself among plants and piles of records. He

7

slept soundly in the sun, only occasionally rattling a paper or toppling a plant as he shifted positions.

Greg was off on Saturdays, and Clancy spent that entire day in the office. He was so well behaved that gradually he came to stay with us a few days during the week. To encourage him to remain in his corner during clinic I left a water bowl, canned food and dry food within easy reach. But all too often when Greg was concentrating on a patient's X ray, Clancy, a noisy eater, would interrupt with a crunch or slurp.

Still, as time went on Clancy was allowed five-day access to the office, although Greg never actually acknowledged the concession.

Some afternoons Clancy would sit in Greg's office across the hall. While Greg worked at his desk Clancy slept curled up on the extra chair. But as soon as Greg left the office for a few minutes Clancy jumped down, stretched, and then took possession of Greg's chair, which he clearly preferred. When Greg returned, he always displaced Clancy from the chair, but he never threw him out of the office. And sometimes I would catch Greg reaching over and gently petting the slumbering beast.

The song that Clancy purred to me the first night he entered my life became a vital part of my days for the next two years. His former owners never called or came to visit Clancy. I guess they thought that any contact with him would be too painful for them. He was my cat now, and we spent our days learning about one another. Those days were precious days, bonus days for Clancy and me.

I learned one thing quickly about Clancy: he could not be trusted. I had completed morning treatments in time for clinic, despite my late start that morning. Greg walked back into the office and glanced at Clancy.

"Samantha, your cat's into something, again."

I reached over to extract the string or other inedible that he always finds, just as my eyes fell on the overturned shoe box. My fingers had already grasped the slimy object in his mouth when I realized that it was the partially devoured tail and hindquarters of Greg's mouse. "Clancy, that's terrible."

But Clancy disagreed. He strode boldly to his sunny den, stretched his stocky legs, and concentrated on cleaning his right front paw.

Chapter 2

Oncology has daily clinics on the eighth floor. I work with a team of three doctors, treating animals who have cancer. As research associate with the unit, I work in clinic, treat our hospital patients, and participate in any special projects or studies involving cats. I maintain records for the unit and assist in compiling data, writing, and editing publications.

The clinic was always busy, and I learned by listening to the doctors and by watching their examinations what questions were pertinent. Some of the doctors were especially patient in answering my questions when I first began working. They explained the tests that they ran, the diagnoses they made, and the treatments they prescribed. Most of our animals are seen on an out-patient basis. We see as many as 125 patients a week, and 75 percent are rechecks or scheduled treatment visits.

The waiting room decor is limited to a few plants. The room itself needs painting, but the painting must wait until the ceiling tiles are replaced, and these will only be replaced when the air-conditioning and heating units are repaired. Still, there is a lovely view of the Fifty-ninth Street Bridge and the East River. We can see the helicopters land across the street.

We have three examination booths which open onto the waiting room. They are separated by partitions that begin six inches from the floor and extend only partway to the ceiling.

Each day has basically the same beginning, but each day holds the promise of a few new faces, a hundred possibilities, and perhaps one miracle.

Monica Cosgrove was sitting with Mykonos when I walked into the waiting room.

"Which is heavier," I asked, "Mykonos or his record?"

"His record is heavier than he was when we first came here, but now I think he's got it beat!"

Mykonos was a large white Persian who had been coming in periodically for two years for treatment. He was sent to us originally as a possible cancer patient. Monica had taken him to several doctors when he began to have diarrhea. She had changed doctors and treatments in desperation as he continued to lose weight. She had watched helplessly as he grew weaker, and she had gained no support from friends who advised her to euthanize the poor cat. She could not end his life without knowing for certain that she could not help him. Finally one of the doctors in our general clinic on the second floor examined him and discovered thickened intestinal loops

11

and an enlarged abdominal lymph node. He performed some tests that indicated that Mykonos might have cancer, and referred him to Oncology. We repeated the tests and found that Mykonos had a higher than normal number of white blood cells in his peripheral blood and bone marrow. An abnormal percentage of these cells were eosinophils.

Eosinophils are white blood cells produced in response to allergies, parasite infestation or any foreign stimulation. We biopsied the thickened part of Mykonos's intestine and the enlarged abdominal lymph node, removing a small piece of tissue for examination. The results indicated that his intestines were inflamed, but we didn't know why.

Mykonos did not have cancer. What he needed was treatment to stop the abnormal production of eosinophils that was aggravating his condition. We treated him with chemotherapy, and within five months his abdomen was normal and so were his blood tests.

Mykonos was sprawled on the table while Audrey finished examining him.

"No diarrhea?" she asked.

"He had a little last night," Monica replied. Because of her conscientiousness we knew that we could try to lengthen the intervals between treatments without endangering Mykonos's health. Monica was aware of the subtle shifts in his mood, and she could tell when he was depressed.

"Well, we'll go ahead and treat him, then. I think we'll try to go five weeks again, if his blood test is normal."

"Yes, that seems to be the longest possible interval right now," she agreed.

We took the blood sample from his hind leg. The blood test would show us whether he had an increased percentage of eosinophils and an elevated white blood cell count; if so, he would need more frequent treatments. I held on to his leg to make sure that he wasn't bleeding once the needle was removed. He didn't mind the bloodletting procedure as much as the protective measures that followed.

"Hold on, sir," I requested as he attempted to pull his leg away. "I'll give it back to you, although I must admit, I like this foot very much."

As the Cosgroves left, Greg was seeing Tabby Rodolitz in another booth. She was an eighteen-year-old calico cat. Tabby had a recurrent fibrosarcoma on her left front leg. A fibrosarcoma is a malignant growth that develops in fibrous connective tissue. Tabby had undergone surgery twice in two months because the tumor had grown back. The veterinarian who sent her to us felt that he could not completely excise the mass now. The tumor was growing around the tendons and extended as far as the bone. We had tried immunotherapy injections for three months, but the mass continued to grow. As I walked into the room Greg was examining Tabby's leg.

"Mrs. Rodolitz, I think our options are exhausted at this point. The immunotherapy doesn't seem to be working at all, and the mass is too extensive for surgery."

"Why can't we amputate the leg?" asked Mrs. Rodolitz.

"Tabby's eighteen years old, and it's questionable whether she could tolerate the surgery. I really couldn't recommend an amputation on a cat this age."

"But she's healthy otherwise, and she doesn't even use the leg now, so she wouldn't really miss it. I can't put her to sleep, Dr. MacEwen, not without giving her every chance."

I was petting Tabby as they were talking, and smiled as she raised her hindquarters each time I stroked her. She was purring loudly.

13

"She does seem to be in good shape," Dr. MacEwen conceded. "Let's run some blood tests and X rays, and then go from there."

Greg and I went into the office to fill out the radiology request for Tabby.

"What would you do if she were your own cat?" he asked.

"Before I came here, I'm not sure," I replied. "But now I'd have to give her this chance."

Mrs. Rodolitz was an unusual client. Most of our clients feel an immediate aversion to the idea of amputation, believing that the result will be painful for their pets. Since we often understand our cats in terms of our own feelings, it is natural that the idea of amputation creates an image of handicap and readjustment to an altered life-style. But cats are graceful, adaptable animals. They can function normally with three legs, still able to outrun two-legged creatures when they choose. While it is true that a patient may be sore for a few days after surgery, the discomfort is slight compared to the suffering when the tumor is still present and growing. Besides, most of the patients are no longer using the involved leg by the time that we consider surgery.

The owner will not be present to share with us the moment of that first ventured step, or the first meal after surgery. Ambulatory, free from pain, and hungry, the cat is ready to go home. The owner will have the joy of seeing her cat thrive at home. The pain and discomfort are over; the cat makes the adjustment easily. There are no emotional crises to face. Cats don't worry about what other cats will think. They are remarkable survivors.

One owner told me she cringed when her three-legged cat first jumped out of the carrier. She described watching him fall the first time he attempted to reach the counter. Instinctively I touched her arm to hold her back. "Yes," she smiled, "he had to work it out himself. On the second try he made it."

"If she were mine," I told Greg again, "yes, I'd have to try."

Tabby's X rays and blood tests confirmed her health, and she was scheduled for surgery the next day. Our surgeon, Jay Harvey, planned to operate on her early in the morning. She could recover from the anesthesia and from the procedure itself during the rest of the day and, we hoped, go home the following day. I brought her into the ward and found a sunny cage for her.

I thought Jay was one of the finest surgeons at the center. He had trained at the center and then moved to California for a one-year residency program. When he returned, he was interested in specializing in surgical oncology. It was important for the Oncology Unit to work with a surgeon who was aware of the special problems involved in many of our cases. Most of our patients were older dogs and cats. Some of them were being treated for other problems as well, such as diabetes or heart disease, and therefore were considered greater surgical risks. Some of the surgery might cause disfigurement, especially if it involved tumors on the face and in the mouth. Jay had achieved a remarkable balance in his approach to surgery. He would perform an extensive procedure, always remembering that his patient was a pet whose postoperative life must be as normal as possible. He would operate to relieve pain or discomfort even if he could not cure. When he advised against surgery, it was because he believed that he could not help the animal and did not want to subject the pet to an unnecessary operation. He was fast and thorough. More than this, however, he was constantly aware of the patient under the surgical drape. His sense of responsibility didn't end with the operation, and many times we would meet in the recovery room where we both went to check on a patient. We met again at Tabby's cage when she was recovering from anesthesia. Jay had put her under a heat lamp because she was cold after the surgery.

"I think we'll leave her in Intensive Care overnight, just so she'll be watched," he said.

"She's waking up already," I commented as she began moving her hind legs and moaning softly.

"You know we repeated the X rays on her." He smiled. "We couldn't believe the chest films were those of an eighteen-year-old cat. We thought maybe Radiology had mixed up their patients!"

Three hours after surgery Tabby was recovering in Intensive Care. Everyone fussed over her, and through the crowd I saw that she was eating baby food. She went home the next day.

Mrs. Rodolitz waited on the second floor while I brought Tabby out in her carrier. She opened the box, and Tabby trilled to her.

"She's relieved to have that awful mass gone, I think," she commented. Mrs. Rodolitz didn't even seem to notice the shaved fur and the suture line that closed the layers of skin where Tabby's leg had been. She was so happy that Tabby was alive and comfortable that she didn't even ask how soon the fur would grow back.

Tabby continued to climb trees and rule her household for two years. We saw her for periodic rechecks and vaccinations. Tabby's extra years were playful and adventurous, and we were all proud to have been a part of her twenty-year life. Every time that Greg recommended amputation for a cat, he remembered Tabby.

Chapter 3

Toward the end of a busy morning clinic Clancy sat up and yawned. Lately I had noticed that while we worked in clinic, as Clancy grew more confident, Clancy worked on Greg. When the waiting room was full and people were standing out in the hallway, Greg frequently became tense. The change was visible in his face: no smiles, no extraneous comments. Clancy seemed to sense the change even before I did. Stretching his sleepy tiger body, he would stroll down the counter to the spot where Greg was leaning, writing in a record. Clancy would deliberately walk across the record to sit on the other side, with his tail still draped across it. Greg moved the tail. Clancy flicked it back. Greg moved the record. Clancy shifted his position. Greg put down the pen and considered throwing Clancy on the floor. Clancy whipped the pen off the counter with his tail and sauntered back to the window. The tension was broken, and Greg almost always smiled. If Clancy was wrong, he ended up back in his cage, but I guess he felt it was worth the gamble.

I was in the ward that afternoon when Greg walked in. The ward houses twenty-eight medium-size stainless steel cages, twelve smaller cages, and a large run. One bank of fourteen cages and the run overlook the river. In the morning the sun enters every cage on one side of the ward, and I always try to admit animals to that side.

"Sam, I need a cage for a cat I examined last night," Greg said. Some of the doctors worked in private practice on their evenings off from the Animal Medical Center. "He's going to stay with us for a while. He has a bloody pleural effusion and is very easily stressed," he explained. A pleural effusion is the accumulation of fluid in the chest cavity. The pressure from the fluid can compress the lungs and cause the animal breathing difficulty.

"Why don't his owners want to keep him?" I asked, for they were donating the cat to us.

"They have thirty-some dogs and cats already, and they really can't afford to pursue a diagnosis, especially when it doesn't look very promising. He's been losing weight, and he's not even eating now. They wanted to give him a chance, but they can't keep him."

It was not unusual for our Animal Medical Center clients to have more dogs and cats than they might have originally set as their limit. The people who care enough to ensure the well-being of their pets also frequently can't ignore a stray or injured pet. Apartment living generally restricts the number, however. In our new patient's case food and shelter were not enough. Moreover, it was possible that his illness was contagious and might endanger the health of the other cats. A large number of animals in a limited space is an unhealthy, stressful situation for the animals and their would-be protectors.

Siggie arrived in a cardboard pet carrier that said "I'm going home." Greg was opening the carrier and I saw the tiger stripes. "Oh, he's so"—at this point the cat looked up at me—"long," I finished. Perhaps because of his thinness his length seemed exaggerated. His Roman nose only added to the impression. He was trembling. He looked worried and intense beyond his three years. As I put him in his cage he seemed to disappear against the wall.

Greg suspected that Siggie had a mass in his chest that was pressing against the esophagus to cause gagging and vomiting. Siggie's history, age, and symptoms were suggestive of lymphosarcoma, a malignant tumor involving the lymph glands. We submitted blood samples and the fluid that we had removed from his chest. Radiographs confirmed the presence of a mass above his heart. Then we waited for the results.

The tests revealed that Siggie did not have feline leukemia or lymphosarcoma. We still didn't know what he did have. He continued to lose weight and to sit trembling in his cage. When he did eat, he vomited. I walked in as Greg and Audrey were reviewing Siggie's record a week after he had arrived.

"Greg, I think we have to consider surgery before he gets too weak. We can't treat him without a diagnosis, and he can't go much longer without treatment."

"I think you're right, Audrey, but we also have to consider expenses at this point. A thoracotomy is a major procedure, and we can't be sure that his disease is treatable even with a diagnosis."

An exploratory thoracotomy would involve opening Siggie's chest to determine what was causing his problems. If the surgeons felt that they could remove the mass, which we were hoping was the thymus, then the procedure would become a thymectomy. If the mass was more diffuse and involved lymph nodes or was in itself too extensive to remove, then they would biopsy it, removing what they could, close him up, and await the pathology results.

"Who's going to pay for this?" Greg continued. "The unit has paid the bill so far, but we have to be realistic. The cat doesn't belong to anyone. We may have to get our diagnosis at postmortem."

But for seven days I had fed and cared for this trembling, pathetic Siggie cat. I had grown fond of him, and he was responding to my attention. Holding the striped bundle in my arms, I turned to them.

"Listen," I began, "I have this cat who needs a thoracotomy."

They smiled, looking relieved.

"We'll get Jay to do it tomorrow."

Jay was not scheduled for surgery the next day, but he spoke to Dr. Steve Withrow, a second-year surgical resident. Steve was interested in oncology cases and worked closely with the unit. It was a two-man procedure, and he and Jay arranged their schedules to accommodate Siggie and his new owner.

I asked Jay to let me help anesthetize Siggie, because he was such a nervous patient. The surgical area was new to him, and I thought that he might feel more secure if he knew I was there. Jay asked if I wanted to stay during the procedure, and I accepted. I was nervous and silent as I sat and watched the machine that recorded Siggie's heartbeat. Finally I heard Steve's voice. "It looks good, Sam. I think I can get the whole thing." I knew he was smiling through his surgical mask. They removed the mass from Siggie's chest and submitted it for histologic diagnosis. Siggie went to Intensive Care, and while he recovered from the anesthesia I went home.

Living so close to the hospital enables me to stop by any evening to check on a patient. I love being able to do this. But it is being home that allows me time and space apart from my work. Time to think things out, to balance my life with other interests, to widen the channels of experience that, at the hospital, so often end in death. Here at home I am living with diversity. I am worker, student, daughter, friend. I am independently the head of a household. Home allows me the precious time to remember, to feel, and to dream. Home is the world that I share with my own four cats. I return every day to Natasha, Daphne, Frederick, and Sam. They delight me with their antics, discovering old toys and new tricks. Grooming one another or stretching between naps, they reassure me with their well-being. They comfort and strengthen me with their love.

Sometimes my cave, sometimes my castle, home is where they are. And soon Siggie would be a part of that refuge.

When I returned that night, Jay had already visited him and tried to feed him. Siggie waited, however, and when I came, he ate some baby food and purred for my benefit. The mass removed was a thymoma, a benign growth involving the thymus, and an extremely rare occurrence in cats.

After I brought Siggie home, I took a few days off from work to be with him. He no longer trembled and was eating voraciously. He adjusted well to my other cats, but then he had had a lot of practice in his other home. Siggie is now a sixteen-pound, glossy-coated tiger with a very long nose. He is eleven years old.

Natasha, Daphne, Frederick, and I moved to our present home a year after I began working at the center. The former tenant left me his cat, Sam, to care for temporarily while he got settled in California. But he never really got settled, and so Sam became a permanent member of our household. The two girls and he ignored each other, but Sam and Frederick immediately fought for dominant male status. They are equal in size, each weighing fifteen pounds. Frederick is gray and black tiger-striped with a spotted stomach, and Sam looks like a lumbering polar bear, all white with a few streaks of silver on his forehead. After all these years they have not stabilized the arrangements and periodically revive the controversy. Frederick was declawed by his former owner; my other cats are not. Some of the most difficult cats that we work with at the hospital are declawed. Their aggressive behavior is probably intended to mask the fact that they feel defenseless. I think that is why Frederick behaves as he does toward Sam.

When Siggie came home, he and Frederick recognized one another as brothers of the tiger-striped clan. Perhaps because of his diminished physique Siggie was not a threat to Sam. In fact, Siggie served as a buffer. At night Natasha slept by my right foot, Daphne at my neck, Frederick and Sam at my left foot with Siggie sandwiched between them.

On my second day home I wandered over to the center to visit Clancy. This was the first time that I had been away from him for more than a weekend, and I missed him. I also knew that Greg would not let him out when I wasn't there.

Greg made security checks to impede any escape attempts.

Clancy meowed when he saw me, but remained in the back of his cage. Even when I opened the door, he lay still. He had not eaten. I looked at his record and saw that he had a fever. Greg had noted his abnormal behavior. Clancy was sitting in a corner of his cage with his back to the door, meowing. I took him into the office, and he seemed content to sit with me while I talked to him. I fed him, and he ate.

The next day his temperature and appetite were normal. He ignored me. If he was ill, he had recovered quickly; if he disliked the interruption of his daily routine, it was now reinstated. I was learning that I was an integral factor in determining the quality of his days.

Quality became a meaningful word in my experience at the center. It was the word that best explained why I worked in the Cancer Therapy Unit. Quality was the factor that balanced significantly against death. Cancer therapy was not only a means of delaying death; it was an effort to ensure the quality of life. Ten minutes of therapy a week could enable a cat to breathe normally, to eat without vomiting, to walk using hind legs that had been paralyzed.

Quality meant dealing with the cat's illness one day a week and concentrating on the cat for the remaining six. It meant the smile on a client's face when the X rays were free of evidence of any spread of the disease. It meant expanding the intervals between treatments and, in some cases, stopping treatment completely.

My family and friends are sometimes confused by my involvement in my work. They accept the fact that I believe in what the unit is working for, but I don't think they really understand why. I tried to tell them about Tabby's surgery, but most of them stopped listening when I mentioned that she was eighteen. They thought her too old for such a procedure. When I spoke about Siggie before we knew what his fate would be, most of my friends were distressed that a sick cat had to face surgery. He was too young to endure such an ordeal.

Perhaps their reaction is intended as a warning against my obvious involvement. I try to tell them about our owners' commitment. Owners are even more involved in the care of their pets. They arrange their schedule for treatments, give medication at home, notice behavior changes, and love their pets. The owners entrust their animals' medical care to us. How can I not become involved when an owner is willing to make this commitment?

Cancer, unlike politics and religion, is not a topic of controversy. No one is for it. But cancer is not another word for death. Neither is it a single illness for which there is one cure. Instead it takes many forms, and each form responds differently to treatment. There are stories of failures and the painful decisions that love demands. But there are also stories of cats with cancer who gain weight, who play and groom themselves, eat plants, and go to the country on weekends. For as long as they are happy.

In many cases we give our clients an average survival time, which is merely an estimate to help the client understand the prognosis. But what excites and encourages me is the cat who goes into remission and gains weight, who never experiences adverse drug reactions, and who sails past our average survival time without a pause.

Our patients have remarkable dignity. We cannot help all of them live long lives, but we can help many of them live good lives. Each one deserves the expertise of our unit and, even more, individual attention and concern. I work with cancer patients because they deserve someone who wants to be there with them. I want them to feel as safe, as comfortable, and as respected as they can in a hospital situation.

Quality is not duration or endurance. It is a timeless, elusive commodity. It is a word that, more than defining life, we strive to make synonymous with life for every patient.

Chapter 4

When the first snow fell in December I opened the window to bring a handful of nature inside for my cats. Daphne, the classic mischievous feline, attempted to get out through the open window. As soon as her front paws touched the cold, wet fire escape she reconsidered.

I've been careful about screenless windows since Natasha disappeared years ago. A friend was staying at my old apartment while I was away for the weekend, and he promised to take care of Daphne and Natasha. When I returned, he was out. Daphne met me at the door, ran past me into the hall, and headed for the staircase. I called her, and she pranced into the apartment, delighted with herself. I looked for Natasha, surprised that she was not at the door. Seeing my open window by the fire escape, I didn't wait for my friend's return. My next-door neighbor was out, but I thought that Tasha had most likely walked across the fire escape into his open window. I called her name through the closed door but didn't hear a reply. I climbed the stairs, remembering that Daphne, each time she ran into the hall, ran for the stairs leading up. I knocked on doors, but most people were at work. Those who were home had not seen her. The door to the roof was open, and I walked out.

The tar was soft beneath my feet, hot from the sun. On the roof of the building attached to mine a woman was hanging up her laundry to dry.

"What are you looking for, dear?" she asked when she observed me searching the roof, calling for Natasha.

"My cat," I replied. "My cat's gone." I was frightened now and verging on tears.

"What does she look like?" she asked. "Is she white and orange and—"

"And black," I said, completing her description of my calico. "Where is she?"

"I found her in the hall of my building," she explained. "I couldn't pick her up. But when I opened my door she came in."

I was so relieved that I interrupted again. "Will you take me to her?"

"Well, she's not there. This morning my husband opened the door, and she ran out. He saw her run up the stairs to the roof again."

I returned to my building and found that my weekend guest had returned. He had spoken to the man next door, who confirmed my original surmise. Natasha had entered his apartment through the open window. He simply opened the front door and let her out into the hall.

I checked outside the building, reluctantly looking in the backyard in case she had fallen from the roof. Relieved at not finding her there, I returned to my apartment and waited for my neighbors to return.

I was furious at my friend. I never left my windows open wide, and I always closed them when I left the apartment. Before I worked at the center, I closed the windows primarily as a precautionary measure. My apartment faced the back and was accessible by the fire escape. When I started working at the center, I discovered a more important reason for being careful.

We call them high-rise cats. These are the cats who fall off window ledges or fire escapes when their owners assume that cats, being graceful creatures, will not lose their balance. A bird, a loud noise, a sudden movement can startle them, and in that moment of distraction they fall. Some of them recover, depending upon how far they fell, how they landed, and what broke their fall. Many of them die.

I was explaining this to my guilty friend when we heard a commotion in the hall. A lovely old Italian lady who didn't speak English lived diagonally across from me. Her door was open, and she was in the hall trying to summon help. We ran to assist her, and she pulled me into her apartment, over to a large carved wooden wardrobe. I heard Natasha meow. As soon as she heard my voice she came out.

I don't know what my Italian lady expected to find, but she smiled when she saw Natasha. I imagine that she had heard my frightened kitty move or perhaps had seen movement without realizing how domestic her intruder was. We all returned to our proper homes, and my friend found new lodgings elsewhere.

Daphne didn't like lectures and concentrated on washing the dirty snow from her immaculate paws.

On Christmas Eve we finished clinic and met in the office to share good wishes and a drink. Monica Cosgrove had sent us six bottles of French champagne, as she had every year since Mykonos became our patient. The card read, "Thank you for another year." We opened a bottle.

Clancy loved Christmas. He loved the presents, loved sampling the food and then the boxes it was packaged in. He always managed to fit, no matter what the size. But as the days had grown shorter this year he had seemed to be slowing down. He still demanded to be out with his public, but he was less conspicuous. We found nothing specifically wrong with him, yet he was changing.

"Clancy didn't eat today," I mentioned as I opened a can of Super Supper, his favorite.

"I left my lunch out on the counter the other day, and he didn't touch it." Jay had previously shared his lunch unintentionally with Clancy, who had torn open the tinfoil, dragged out the roast beef, and rolled the apple under Jay's desk.

I watched as Audrey picked him up and examined him. She glanced at Greg and laughed nervously, as she does when she is uncomfortable or upset. Greg confirmed her findings. Clancy's kidneys were enlarged and irregular. He was still leukemia test positive. He was seven. I knew that lymphosarcoma involving the kidneys was a likely diagnosis. Jay walked over and put his arm around me. "We'll take care of him, Sam, don't worry. We're a pretty good team, aren't we?" I smiled back at him. Audrey had her coat on, and Jay went to get his.

"Merry Christmas. See you Friday." Greg reached over and patted the tiger-striped head. "Good night, old man."

I took the quilted blanket that I had made for Clancy and placed it beside him in the corner. His name was embroidered in green against the brown-and-mint paisley pattern. I kissed him on the striped M on his forehead, and he pretended to be sound asleep.

"It's okay, Clancy, you don't have to con me tonight. Merry Christmas, angel." I turned out the lights and locked the door. No one complained that he was not in his cage.

Christmas Eve was my favorite day of the year. I had celebrated in various ways over the years, at parties, with friends, or at concerts. But no matter where I was or with whom, I always wanted to be home on Christmas Eve.

This year was ending, and I felt my carefree days with Clancy slipping away. On this special night of sorrow and joy, of quiet wonder and peace, I went home to Natasha and Daphne, Frederick, Siggie, and Sam. Home was where I needed to be.

Christmas Day Audrey came in to check our hospital cases and to take phone calls. Even on holidays the clients are able to speak to a doctor on all services. In Oncology the three doctors alternated holidays, and Christmas was Audrey's turn. When she arrived, I had already fed Clancy. He ate a jar of beef baby food, and I gave him a special treat of roast beef. Then Audrey and I distributed the catnip mice that we had bought to the cats in the ward. Clancy got a blue mouse, but I think that he would have preferred the real thing.

I went home and opened three cans of Turkey and Giblets for my family's Christmas dinner, thinking that this was a traditional choice for the occasion. Only Siggie was grateful. Natasha presented herself appropriately in a Bloomingdale's box under the tree while Daphne removed the ornaments from the lower branches. Frederick and Sam seemed to respect the holiday cease-fire. Siggie ate everyone's food.

Chapter 5

Christmas was over. On Friday routine was reinstated at the center, and we scheduled Clancy for his biopsy. I sat with him in the recovery room, and many of his admirers stopped by to visit him. Jay had biopsied his kidneys. Clancy had lymphosarcoma. He was not a stoic patient, but he reserved his complaints for an audience. Left alone, he dozed. I carried him back to the eighth floor to his cage, where he would receive intravenous fluid therapy. He was exhausted and showed no reluctance to remain in his cage. When I left for the day, he was sleeping in his litter pan, and his fluid bottle was set up outside the cage for his night's treatment. At two o'clock the next morning the phone rang in my apartment.

"Samantha? This is AnneMarie." She was a night treatment nurse. "Do you have Clancy with you?"

"No—he's missing? But he was hooked up to fluids."

"Well, the bottle is there, but the connection tube is broken. His cage door was open when I came up to check him."

"He's not in the ward? Maybe someone put him in another cage."

"No, I checked the ward, and I've been calling up and down the hall for him. I thought maybe you had him, or that you'd know his hiding places."

"But he had surgery today," I reasoned. "He couldn't go far. I'll be right over."

"Samantha, how could he get outside the ward with the door closed?"

"I don't know. I've never known." I smiled as I pictured him sleeping soundly in his cage. He had outfoxed me again.

As I walked down the hill to the hospital I tried to outline a plan. His favorite spot was the storage area down the hall, but it was locked at night. I always had thought it was his favorite place because of the hysteria he created whenever Harold, the supply manager, who was wary of cats, saw him in there.

I checked the ward again and the office. Calling his name, I walked down the hall. A distant meow drew me to the storage room. As I continued calling his name his cries became louder and more urgent. A flashlight shone on two round eyes, and familiarity gave form to the surrounding darkness. Clancy had climbed the ten-foot grating and was sitting on the top shelf of the storage wall, insisting that he could not come down. After all, he was sick.

I rescued my little soldier, and he purred while I yelled and cried. That morning Harold complained that someone had torn into two fifty-pound bags of dry food, from the bottom.

We waited a week after Clancy's surgery to allow healing of the biopsy site. On January 2 we began treatment. Clancy growled and hissed, fighting his weekly chemotherapy treatments. But five minutes of discomfort for all of us was worth the change in him once his treatments began. Within a week after his first treatment his kidneys became smaller and his appetite increased. He was playful and curious again.

The beginning of each new year was a time of reflection for me. After the excitement of Christmas I found myself thinking back instead of anticipating the future. Subdued, reflective, and perhaps a little melancholy.

I was at home taking my tree down, kneeling on the floor and packing the surviving ornaments in boxes when I felt two paws on the back of my neck. I spun around and Frederick reached up again, standing on his hind legs, and hugged me. He had taught me that this gesture meant "pick me up," and he purred his approval. Is that what he had done in his former home? I wondered how his previous owner could have given him up. This magnificent tiger was brought to the hospital to be euthanized because his owner's fiancée was allergic to cats. He was a healthy adult cat whose life was almost terminated because his owner had made a choice.

I wondered about the previous life-styles of my adopted adult cats. They seemed to adjust quickly to the new environment, but I wondered about their kittenhood and their previous daily routines.

When I moved to my present apartment, Natasha and Daphne stretched as though it was the first time in their lives that they had had enough room. All the cats loved the space in the new apartment. I don't know how large Siggie's former place was, but he now galloped the length of his home, usually around 1 A.M., three or four times a week. In the old two-room apartment Natasha used to bring items from my laundry bag up the steps to my loft bed. Now when I had company, she could drag underwear from the bathroom, through five rooms, and drop it at the foot of my guest.

Sometimes at work I watched Clancy in a new situation, amazed at his adaptability. One of the television stations filmed a segment in the waiting room for a news program. They arrived after clinic, and Greg had arranged a late appointment for a dog with mammary gland tumors. When Greg finished the examination, there was still time for another segment. Clancy was helping the camera crew, jumping on boxes and examining their equipment. I suggested making him a TV star. Greg thought that we could pretend to give Clancy his treatment. I placed the star on the exam table. Lights, camera, and action as Greg reached for Clancy's leg, needle in hand. Clancy knew that he had just been treated the day before. He showed the film crew what a terrible experience this was for a helpless kitty. We finally settled for an episode showing Greg listening to Clancy's heart. Greg's head was bowed as Clancy looked straight into the camera.

Clancy, the star, made full use of the eighth floor accommodations. It was difficult to believe that he had once stayed in a cage for most of the day. He might stop by to visit Greg or wander down the hall to torment Harold.

Once when I went down to retrieve Clancy, Harold said, almost accusingly, "I thought you said he was sick." In his own way I think Harold actually cared. Clancy, with his stubborn perseverance, had conquered another heart. Harold let him sit in empty boxes and climb the mountains that appeared with each delivery. Only when Clancy got underfoot or when he maneuvered toward the dry food bags did Harold summon my assistance.

The new year had offered Clancy and me a compromise. Our careless routine was disrupted and a new one introduced. We would endure weekly therapy, and the weekly reminder that our lives had been altered. It was a compromise, but we accepted the terms. As much as I resisted it, change had worked its way into my routine.

The new year brought with it new faces, new names, new stories. The clinic waiting room was a mixture of familiar and unfamiliar faces, and cats whose visits I would soon begin to anticipate.

Mr. and Mrs. Berkeley were visiting our clinic for the first time. Denton was a nine-year-old black cat who had undergone a mastectomy elsewhere nine months ago. Jay and I went in to meet Denton and her owners.

"Do we know what the original biopsy was?" Jay asked as he examined her.

"The doctor said it was malignant," Mr. Berkeley replied.

"Well, she has recurrence along her mammary glands, and it feels as though it might have spread to her axillary lymph nodes."

"We were afraid it might have spread."

"We can take her to surgery, But I don't know if—"

"No," Mrs. Berkeley interrupted. It was the first time she had spoken. "No more surgery."

"Well," Jay continued, "I don't know if we could remove all the tumor, and I think she might have some problems healing in that area."

I knew that Jay would not insist upon surgery. If he believed that he could best help Denton by surgical removal of her tumor, he would have explained the procedure and the effect of the surgery on Denton's prognosis so that the Berkeleys could think about it. The tumor was in a difficult location, however, and Jay was concerned that not only might he not be able to remove it all, but also that the surgery might help spread the disease.

"Why don't we start her on immunotherapy today?" he suggested. "A series of sixteen weekly injections. Maybe this boost of her immune system will help to keep these tumors under control."

"Will she get sick from the treatment?" Mrs. Berkeley asked.

"Most of our cats don't. They seem to tolerate the therapy well. Some of them run a fever. Some may be depressed for a few hours after or not feel like eating, but usually they're fine by that night or the next morning. We'll monitor her response and find the best dosage for her. I think that's the best plan that we can offer you. We don't recommend using chemotherapy in cats with mammary tumors, because our results haven't been encouraging."

"No, we don't want to give her chemotherapy."

Mrs. Berkeley's reaction was not uncommon in our clinic. When I began working in the unit, we were using chemotherapy primarily on dogs. I was afraid of these drugs that killed both normal and abnormal cells. I was apprehensive about possible toxic effects, even though the dogs tolerated therapy well. Cats are not little dogs, however, and medication often affects them differently.

The first cat we treated with chemotherapy had lymphosarcoma and was leukemia test positive. I remember standing and watching him after his treatment, waiting for something to happen. What happened within twenty-four hours was that his chest mass decreased in size and his appetite increased.

I am still apprehensive about chemotherapy, although I am aware of its effectiveness. I worry about the effects of long-term therapy, recognizing that this concern in itself is a sign of our progress in treating disease. Chemotherapy is rarely a cure for our patients, but in many cases it provides valuable time. In some cases it enables us to combine therapy modes, shrinking a tumor mass enough, for example, for us to consider surgery that was previously impossible.

Most of our clients had personally observed the effects of chemotherapy on a friend or had heard tragic stories about such treatment. In human medicine they use much higher doses, and that may be one reason that their results are much better than ours. They aim for a cure, while we try to control the disease. We can't subject the owner or the cat to a helpless situation. We try to maintain the quality of the cat's life. In Denton's case more aggressive therapy with either surgery or drugs would certainly cause immediate discomfort for her, and would probably not ensure her a longer or better life.

There are certain disease forms that don't respond to conventional therapy. New modes of therapy can offer hope when we have nothing else to give. Our clients are informed about the possible consequences of therapy and advised of all the alternatives available. If one form of treatment works well in most cases, the client should be informed of that. Our patients aren't experimental animals. They are pets, and we believe that we owe them and their owners the benefit of our experience. We have enough diseases that don't respond to conventional therapy. Many owners are willing to try something new on the chance that it might work. But the choice must be theirs. And the decision has to be based on all the available information.

"She's your cat, isn't she, Mrs. Berkeley?" I asked, smiling at Denton's dependence on her. The golden eyes had not looked away from her face.

"Yes, we've been through a lot together."

I never saw Mrs. Berkeley again. Her husband brought Denton in every week, and during those visits we learned the history of their close relationship. Denton and Mrs. Berkeley were both diagnosed as having malignant breast tumors in March of the previous year. Mrs. Berkeley received chemotherapy and spent a lot of time at home with Denton. The treatments made her terribly ill. When they both had recurrences, Mrs. Berkeley wanted therapy for Denton, but only if it had minimal side effects. For three months Denton did quite well on this treatment, and both the Berkeleys were encouraged.

On a Saturday morning in late April I walked into the waiting room and saw Mr. Berkeley sitting there.

"Are you all right?" I asked him. He looked so tired.

"It's my wife," he started. "They took her to the hospital Thursday. She was so weak, and the treatments—they weren't working anymore."

"They can care for her better in the hospital," I said, "and they can make her more comfortable."

"But I don't know what to do," he said, his voice trembling. "I don't think they can help her. And now Denton."

"Why, what's wrong with Denton?"

"She stopped eating on Thursday, and she's been hiding under my wife's bed. She sleeps there all day."

I lifted the lid of the carrier and gently stroked Denton's black coat. She had lost weight and was breathing heavily.

"Dr. Harvey will be in shortly," I told him. "We'll find out what's wrong with Denton."

When Jay arrived I had the radiology request ready, and

he examined Denton briefly before sending her down for films.

Denton had metastatic lesions and fluid in her lungs. This meant that the cancer cells responsible for the growth in her mammary glands and in the adjacent lymph nodes had now started to grow in her lungs. Mr. Berkeley asked us to euthanize her. He stopped at the door and looked for one last time at Denton.

"She was my wife's cat, you know. Such a comfort to her. I don't think I can tell her."

Mrs. Berkeley died in the hospital three days later.

Some of our regular clients asked about Mr. Berkeley and Denton. They came in on the same day and usually chatted while awaiting their appointments. Our clients who were considering therapy were often aided in making their decisions by seeing other cats who were receiving treatment.

Mr. Berkeley had met a cat with mammary gland cancer who, after five years of therapy, now only came in every six weeks. He had met another black cat who had been coming in for three years after the owner's original doctor had suggested euthanizing the cat. But he also met a man with a Siamese cat that was not responding to therapy. Mr. Berkeley was in the waiting room when we euthanized that wonderful little Siamese.

Most of the friendships formed in the waiting room during those weekly visits didn't continue outside the hospital, but for a short time every week our clients were surrounded by other people who were committed to their animals. Perhaps the boss didn't understand why this employee had to take the cat in once a week, but the person sitting next to him on the waiting-room bench did.

Chapter 6

In February a new educational program started at the center. Students from the University of Maine came to participate in a work-study semester at the hospital. They were studying to become veterinary assistants and technicians. Lectures were given by the AMC doctors, but most valuable was the daily experience that the students gained from working in various areas of the hospital. The first group consisted of eight young women, and they were housed in a small apartment on the eighth floor. The apartment was located at the opposite end of the hall from our ward, next to the supply area. They had three small bedrooms furnished with bunk beds, and a kitchen. Across the hall was a living room with a desk, a sofa, a few chairs, and a television.

Clancy welcomed that first group of students in February,

pleased to share his new living quarters with them. What a remembered joy it must have been for him to sleep on a bed once again. He shared his wondrous self with all the girls. I found him on a different bed each time I came in to reclaim him. I suppose I could have been jealous, but Clancy made everyone feel special. He always acknowledged me with a trill, throwing back his head as though shaking an invisible mane. Sometimes he wandered back to the office on his own. He still slept in his cage at night, but now he had TV privileges. One of the students usually returned him to the ward, but I was not surprised, knowing Clancy's tactics, to find that occasionally he spent the night with the girls.

Day after day I watched his stocky legs carry those familiar tiger stripes past Greg's office and on down the hall. From the office I could hear the welcome he received, almost a daily ovation just for being Clancy.

Clancy was not a performing cat in the traditional sense. He watched me roll balls across the floor, fetch them, and roll them again. He watched me bounce them off the wall. He watched me lose them under the cabinets.

I bought him a mouse collection. Clancy had catnip mice, mice on wheels, battery-operated mice. He had fuzzy mice and rubber mice. He had mice in paisley, stripes, and solid colors. But Clancy knew the real thing.

I gave him a jumping frog, a chicken that pecked along the floor. I bought him a rubber fish and put it in his water bowl. Clancy watched me play with all my new toys. But the fish was too much. He walked over to his bowl to quench his thirst after a morning nap in the glaring sun, only to find something floating in his water. He looked at me as though I had offered meat loaf to a vegetarian. With his two-syllable meow, the one he used for urgency, he reiterated his disapproval. Clancy left the room, and, ashamed, I reeled in the fish.

The one game that he would play with me was itsy-bitsy spider. As Clancy slept in the corner on the counter the five-legged spider of my right hand would begin creeping toward him, accompanied by an a capella solo. He watched as it drew closer. He watched, showing no sign of participation. Finally, when the spider was within reach and I was convinced of Clancy's boredom, he grabbed the five-legged monster with both front paws and sank his teeth into its fleshy center.

The weeks flew by as Clancy made room in his life for all his admirers. He managed to please each one, finding time in his busy daily schedule to single us out for a few special moments.

On a Wednesday in April I saw Mrs. Smith in our clinic waiting room.

"Why don't you bring Oliver Cromwell in and we'll take a look at him," Audrey said. Mrs. Smith picked up the carrier and brought it into the exam room. Oliver was a normal cat who was feline leukemia test positive. We examined him every two or three months because, like Clancy, he was more susceptible to disease. We hoped that these routine examinations would enable us to detect any subtle changes in his physical condition and his blood profile. These periodic checkups also removed some of the pressure from Mrs. Smith. She knew that Oliver was a high-risk candidate for lymphosarcoma, and we all felt better about watching him closely.

Oliver was an impressive cat. He was tiger-striped like Clancy, but he had white markings on his coat.

"How was his last blood test, Dr. Hayes?" Mrs. Smith

asked. We had checked a complete blood count, looking specifically at the numbers of red and white blood cells. Too few white blood cells will not allow the cat to fight infection; too many may indicate the presence of a severe infection or of leukemia.

"Well, his white blood cell count and differential were normal, and he's not anemic. He's still positive for the leukemia virus."

"Yes, I don't suppose that's going to change," she replied. "It's been a while now since he's been taking those pills, but he seems so healthy."

"He checks out just fine. I can't find anything wrong with him."

"No, he wouldn't get sick now. He's going to Maine next month."

"Why did you bring along Topaze? Any problems?"

"No, but he hasn't been in for a while, and he likes to keep Oliver company. We left the girls at home."

Mrs. Smith and her daughter had four cats. Jenny, Samantha, and Topaze were leukemia test negative. When the Smiths discovered that Oliver was positive, the family had been together for six years. The three other cats were still negative, and although the Smiths knew that there was no guarantee that they would remain negative, they couldn't part with any of them. We put them all on the same therapy as Clancy received and tested them periodically.

They all adored Oliver, for he was the oldest and the most worldly. Every summer the Smiths took them to their home in Belfast, Maine. For Oliver and Topaze, Maine was their natural home. The girls were city cats.

Like Mrs. Smith, many of our clients have more than one cat and so we get to meet the entire family. We see cats with

44

diabetes, heart disease, and skin disorders, do yearly vaccinations, discuss diet, and sometimes just clean the ears of a patient's littermate.

"May I say hello to Clancy?" Mrs. Smith asked. "He's lost some weight, hasn't he?"

She had not been in since before Christmas, so I told her about Clancy's illness.

I also told her about Clancy's new nightly routine, developed since the Maine students' arrival in February. I returned him to his clean cage at the end of the day. He immediately spilled the water, turned over his litter pan, defecated, and then meowed pitifully. How could I leave him overnight in that pigpen? Of course, I opened the door and picked him up. He sprang from my shoulder, and the chase was on. Every night I would leave him, finally, in a clean, dry, neat cage. And every morning I discovered a cage full of shredded paper. I wondered if he was working with internal security or else preparing confetti for a parade.

"They're alike in many ways, aren't they?" I said, looking from Clancy to Oliver. "Both seemed destined to be women's cats, our protectors."

"Yes," she answered, "they have a certain stoic nature."

"Perhaps it comes with nobility."

She promised to send us a postcard from Maine.

Clancy's birthday was May 17. It would be our third celebration together. The first week in May he became anemic and developed a fever. I had seen enough cats in our clinic to know that Clancy had reached the final stage. We could treat his symptoms, and he might respond temporarily. Greg asked me only once, early in the week, if I wanted to euthanize Clancy. But I had to try to help him. We treated him with blood transfusions and antibiotics for five days. He did not respond.

The Maine students came to visit him and carried him back to their room for short visits as he grew weaker. The nursing staff asked about him, and Harold, noting Clancy's absence, also inquired. I saw each one's concern. I told them he was dying. I felt their pain and mine touch for a moment, merging in our helplessness, and then shatter into separate fragments of grief and loss. How many friends my little fighter had made. How many barriers he had climbed to reach so many hearts.

Greg walked into the office Friday afternoon as I was treating Clancy.

"Did he eat today?" he asked.

"No, he doesn't even want baby food. His temperature just won't come down. It was 104.6 this morning." The normal range for a cat is 100–102.5.

"His kidneys are still small," he said as he examined him. "But he's so pale again."

I sat with Clancy awhile in the office. The door was open, and I thought how far Clancy had come from his early days with us. We never left the door open in those days, because Clancy would disappear for hours. Now he no longer cared. He was uncomfortable, and our treatments had failed. I recalled his one earlier illness, and the promise that I had made him about the quality of his life. My tough Irish rogue had put up quite a battle since Christmas, but looking at him asleep in my arms, I saw how exhausted he was.

"Greg, I don't think Clancy's happy anymore. I think he wants to die."

The tears that I had held back over these past days could be held back no longer once the words were spoken.

46

To choose euthanasia was to take a chance. A chance of missing a miracle. We had saved Clancy's life once, and we had acted in good faith. We had promised him a life different from his former life, but a good one. We had given him days of curiosity and exploration, days of food and rest, and more food, and countless hours in the sun. And he had lived them fully. In return, to my days he had added laughter and joy, fear and occasional anger, and responsibility. He had added love and, now, sorrow. When he became ill, again we had tried to improve his days and to extend their number. We succeeded for a short time. To save his life now, without a miracle, was impossible. We could keep him alive for a short time longer, but we could not restore the quality of his former days. To keep him alive now was not acting in good faith. It was selfish.

Greg prepared the injection, and I carried Clancy in his quilted blanket, his Christmas blanket, into the examination booth. I held him and felt his heart beating against my arm. As long as it beats, I thought, he's still with me. And once it stops, I'll never see him again. Looking in his trusting eyes, I saw him pacing at the elevator, pouting in his cage. I saw him as he was when he was well and happy.

He did not cry or struggle when the needle entered his vein. He died quickly in my arms. Alone in the room I kissed the M on his striped head, and said good-bye.

Chapter 7

When I was growing up in Buffalo, most of my summers were spent working at a camp in Dunkirk, New York, on Lake Erie. My brother was a lifeguard there, and I worked in the kitchen. I was up at 6 A.M. to make hot cereal for two hundred campers. Since I have been living in New York, a longing for space and water has still accompanied the appearance of pussy willows and lilacs in the florist shops, but now I long for the ocean—now I seek the unpredictable moods, the conflict and passion of waves, and the limitless visage of the Atlantic. And late that May after Clancy's death I needed the wordless comfort that a moment of communion promised.

Jay had arranged his schedule so that beginning in May he had weekends off. Throughout the year Oncology had resident AMC doctors rotating through our service. They worked in clinic or with Jay in surgery, depending upon their area of interest, for a month or six weeks. In this way they were introduced to the special problems encountered in oncology, and this brief exposure enabled them to explore their own feelings about working with cancer patients. Dr. Steve Arnoczky was a surgical resident, and he worked Saturday clinics when Jay shifted to a Monday-through-Friday schedule. Steve was thin and over six feet tall. His full-length lab coat fell several inches short of his knees. He had already decided to specialize in orthopedic surgery and was not particularly interested in oncology, but the staff and clients loved working with him. He was always playing jokes on us or making the clients smile.

Steve often had his camera with him to photograph interesting cases for lectures and teaching purposes. In oncology the responses to therapy were sometimes dramatically documented in photographs. One day earlier in the year, when I saw him taking pictures, I had mentioned how much I wanted photographs of some of our ward cats. He came upstairs with me and spent an hour patiently posing each cat, including Clancy. Months had passed, and I had forgotten about our photo session.

A week after Clancy died, I finished working a busy Saturday clinic. I enjoy steady clinics, but this one was hectic. I was preparing medication for one patient, one was waiting to be treated, and a third needed fluids. We had two cats in Radiology who had to be retrieved and another waiting to go down. Everything was getting done, but there was little time for more than what was required. No pleasantries, no ear-rubs for the cats, and no purrs in return. I felt that if one person asked me to do one more thing I might scream. I was already screaming inwardly. Steve noticed my tension and very seriously asked me to run down to the cafeteria to get coffee for him. Just as Clancy could always reach Greg at a crucial moment, Steve made me laugh at myself.

Steve never said anything about Clancy's death, but he helped me through those empty days when my sadness was buried in efficiency, and my sense of loss magnified by moments with our patients. When clinic was over, Steve handed me a package. He had remembered the photographs, and on the top was a beautiful picture of Clancy.

Two weeks after Clancy's death I found my way to the ocean to visit a friend's unused house on Fire Island. On Thursday Audrey had mentioned that her husband was going away that weekend. She had a car and suggested that we take Chico, one of the hospital cats, on a one-day excursion.

Chico was another cat who had been donated to the unit. His owners had brought him to the hospital when they noticed his open-mouthed breathing. He had a mass in his chest that was diagnosed as lymphosarcoma. Chico was unusual because he was leukemia test negative. (The majority of cats with lymphosarcoma in their chests are positive.) Frightened and aggressive at first, he was extremely difficult to handle. He was easily upset and sometimes created his own stress with a resulting shortness of breath. Treatments were not easy to administer, but with patience and minimal handling we found a system.

Chico actually belonged to the daughter in the family, and she had brought him in for treatment for nine months until she went away to school. Her parents did not want the responsibility of caring for him, and so she had asked us if we could help. We agreed to keep him.

Chico responded rapidly to therapy. With chemotherapy

the mass reduced 75 percent in size with his first treatment, and disappeared by the end of the first month.

Audrey drove out to catch the ferry to Fire Island on Friday night, and I picked up Chico from the hospital early Saturday morning on my way to the train. Audrey had left after work and expected a long drive in rush-hour traffic. We were afraid that Chico would become restless and overheated on such a drive. The train was air-conditioned, and he sat in the seat next to me with the front flap of the carrier open on the seat. I had a leash attached to his collar in case he tried to wander.

He seemed content sitting beside me and occasionally left his seat to join me in mine. When the conductor came by, Chico sat nicely in his carrier. I was always concerned when someone wanted to pet Chico because he nipped at fingers unexpectedly. He was being playful, and we who knew him had learned to hold still until he released us, but the natural impulse was to pull back the hand, and that encouraged Chico to tighten his grip. Fortunately the conductor simply nodded at us and walked on.

The ferry was a new experience for both of us. Chico turned his face to the wind, raising his chin slightly. The movement on the water didn't seem to bother him, and the openness of the ferry exposed us fully to the cool early morning air. The combination of a pre-season outing and the forecast of rain left us with an almost empty ferry.

When we reached land, I followed directions to a typical summer beach colony house, looking very much like the others on the dirt road. I saw Audrey sitting on the sun deck that covered half the second floor.

Chico and I explored the house as Audrey pointed out specific rooms. The bedrooms were small, with only a bed and dresser in each. The living room was light and airy with screened windows on three sides. Chico immediately settled in this main room, eying a vase of dried flowers and leaves. The kitchen had not yet been stocked with supplies, so we walked back into town to buy some coffee for us and some food for our companion.

When we got back, the sun came out briefly for Chico's benefit. We walked on the front lawn. We walked and Chico alternately pulled back on the leash, refusing to budge, and bounded on ahead of us, trying to free himself. We had planned to walk down to see the beach, but forty-five minutes later, when it started to rain, we had gotten only as far as the house next door.

Chico insisted upon sniffing each blade of grass, occasionally sampling one before his next cautious step. When the first drops of rain fell, he had discovered a weed and was methodically examining each leafy protrusion. It rained the entire day, and Chico slept in the living room while we read. He slept until he became bored. He chewed the dried branches, finally overturning the vase. We played with him for a while, and then I left the two of them and ventured out in the rain to the beach.

The waves were rough, slashing the beach with powerful gushing sounds. The ocean seemed angry, but the rain felt soft and sympathetic to my walk. As I wandered down the beach the sky grew darker and the day's mood changed. The rain fell more persistently, its coldness causing me to shiver. Thunder sounded in the distance. The waves slapped furiously and the thunder crept closer. When lightning flashed across the sky, it seemed as though the elements were competing. The waves thrashed against the shore as the sky growled and roared, electrified with light. Simultaneously frightened and exhilarated, I returned to the house.

We went into town for dinner, assuring Chico of a kitty bag. Chico slept in Audrey's room, and in the morning we left early to catch the returning ferry.

The horn sounded as the ferry pulled out and chugged from Fire Island to the mainland. Chico sat erect and felt the moisture in the air. His ears back, he waited fearlessly for something to happen. Audrey and I sat on either side of him, sensing his pleasure.

"He hates his leash," she commented.

"What kind of cat is that?" asked a passenger sitting behind us.

"He's part Abyssinian," Audrey replied, "and part unknown."

She was proud of Chico. He resembled a small mountain lion. He wore his black leather collar well.

Jay and Audrey shared custody of Chico, each taking him on alternate weekends. He was a community cat. We all shared the responsibility for his treatments, and the happiness of his well-being. Loving him was easy and rewarding, and for me it was a different kind of relationship than I had had with Clancy. Clancy had been mine, and his death had stunned me, filling my days with emptiness. I loved Chico, but I felt safer knowing that others loved him too.

It took three of us to treat him, and we only got one chance.

"He sounds like a fire engine," I commented as Jay gave him his injection the Friday after our trip.

"Where's the fire, Chico?" Audrey teased.

"He says it's in his eyes," I replied, moving my hand

quickly. Chico had been declawed on his front paws, but his teeth were large and formidable weapons. "Don't bite the nice nurse, Chico," I requested.

He sat up and snorted, then sprang from the table into the office.

"I'll see you around six, Chico," Jay reminded him, heading back to surgery. It was his turn to take him home this weekend.

"Don't forget, Jay. You know what happened last time."

We had left Chico's carrier open in the office so that he would know that he was going away that night. Jay didn't finish surgery until nine, and completely forgot about him. When we arrived the next morning, Chico had shredded the papers on Jay's desk and then used them as his litter box.

That rainy day at Fire Island was my only holiday escape that summer. I understood why New Yorkers flee the city on summer weekends. Summer was my least favorite season in New York. The cats and I were at a constant energy low. On humid days I left the air-conditioner on in the apartment when I went to work. Frederick enjoyed washing his front paws in the water bowl, usually before jumping on my lap, so I left extra bowls of fresh water for the others. We accepted summer as a long transition between spring and fall.

I missed the summers of my past, the summers that were never long enough. I missed the freedom of walking on the grass, of tripping along a winding dirt path broken by gnarled, protruding tree roots, down to the shore of a still unspoiled lake. Such excursions now mean checking train schedules or riding three hours to my destination.

I curbed my spontaneity when the cats became a part of my life. If I went away for more than one day I had to make arrangements for someone to feed them and change the litter.

54

Linda, one of the nurses at the AMC, was my first choice. In addition to meeting their basic needs she spent some time with them. Our ophthalmologist was an equally agreeable choice for the cats, and I returned the favor with her two cats when she went away. It wasn't the responsibility alone that limited my excursions. I missed them, and while it was possible to travel with one cat, it was impossible to choose only one of my five. Taking them all to an unfamiliar place was not a viable alternative.

So we spent the summer awaiting its end. My memories of past summers grew into dreams of the future. But my plans depended upon their being a part of that dream.

Chapter 8

In late July my mother called from Buffalo. She was crying.

"Dad's in the hospital," she began, "and this time I think it's bad."

Three years ago he had been hospitalized for surgery on his hip. The surgery had been postponed when the doctors discovered a suspicious area in his lungs on the X rays. They described their discovery to Mom as a "shadow" on Dad's lungs. They had not used the word *cancer*. When they sent him home after a few more weeks he seemed fine. Mom and Dad had said nothing to my brother and me about the X rays.

During the next three years Dad had been hospitalized several times. The doctors felt that he was strong enough to undergo two surgical procedures on his hip. Subsequently he had used a walker and had fallen a few times.

"What happened, Mom?" I asked.

"He had an attack, like a seizure. And when they took him to the hospital, they said that he has a brain tumor. He wants to see you, dear. He keeps asking for you and Paul."

My brother was married and lived in Wisconsin.

"Do you want me to call Paul?"

"I already did. He said he'll be here tomorrow. Can you come?"

Of course I could.

My father had cancer—a disease I hadn't even thought about before I started working at the center. Since then I had thought about it frequently, but mostly in terms of our patients. I subscribed to several medical journals, both human and veterinary, but even my reading was focused on the treatment of animals. I had heard of cases of my friends' friends or their relatives, but until now cancer had not touched my family directly.

He lay motionless in the hospital bed. Like a doll, he was manipulated into a different position and remained still until someone changed it. I reached for his bony hand and watched the protruding veins. Mom and Paul spoke to one another, occasionally posing a question to the ghostly figure who had brought us all together again. He responded with a grimace, a frown, and sometimes with a voice so fragile it might break. The doctors were busy, the nurses efficient, and he lay helpless on his bed and told us in such a way that he could not endure . . . the pain, the indignity, the loneliness—why could he not die? And we waited, all four, for the time.

We were a close family in many ways, but not an expressive one. Mom was fighting to maintain her self-control, that control that enabled her to work, visit Dad at the hospital, and think about the future, the near future. Paul and I were concerned that the emotions she was holding back would soon overwhelm her. But she had learned from her parents, as we had from ours, the private, individual depth of grief. Our conversations about Mom also served to distract us from that special sorrow that we both felt. We helped Mom by being there, by holding her hand or smiling across the room. We helped her and ourselves by loving her.

After a few days Paul and I returned to our jobs, leaving Mom alone to carry out the vigil. We were all waiting, but for Mom it was the hardest. Every day she witnessed the changes that time was making, changes that destroyed the stability of happier days.

My brother and I both needed to become totally involved in work. I spent long days at the clinic. Hours would pass when I would not think of Dad. I could think of death, I could focus on death as a concept, but I could not think of his death. To think of him was to relive his pain, a mental and physical anguish that I could do nothing to ease. We survivors, we who are left behind, know the frustration of helplessness. We carry on because it does not help if we don't. We function, not out of strength, but in the absence of any alternative. It was only at night, in the sanctuary of my home, that I could sit stroking Siggie, and feel the sorrow in my life.

Dad had shared his joy in music with Paul and me. Sitting in my living room, years from my childhood, hundreds of miles from my first home, with all the distance of life between us, I would listen to the music that he had made a part of my life. I could listen to Mozart or Wagner and think of nothing, clear my mind of any image, any thought. Once that moment was gone, I could cry. Because the music touched something within me, something that my mind would call sorrow—

sorrow at his inability to hear and to share this with me, sorrow for my own finite life, or anguish that the spirit can attain such heights while the body endures such pain. I could cry because things could not be as they were, because things would never again be the same.

Through the early days of August practical Siggie sent me off to work to earn his cat-food money. Linda and I joked about his voracious appetite. His three favorite things were food, Frederick, and me. Frederick and I could haggle for second place in Siggie's heart, but first place was decided by Siggie's stomach.

Natasha was appalled by Siggie's appetite. When I fed them together, Siggie devoured his dinner and then turned to the nearest plate for seconds. Natasha preferred to eat at a distance from Siggie, since she enjoyed a nice, leisurely meal.

I was prepared to share my dinner with the cats if I was brave enough to bring home fish. But one night I left a dish of steamed vegetables on the table when I left the room to answer the telephone. When I returned to the kitchen, I discovered Sam eating my cauliflower and Daphne manipulating an ear of corn with one paw while gnawing at the kernels. They saved the broccoli for me.

Natasha and Siggie responded to my needs, seizing every opportunity to sit with me. Frederick danced on my lap, honoring me by cleaning my arm with his sandpaper tongue. When I could tolerate the ritual no more and displaced him, he sought out Sam for a tumble. Daphne had her own needs. If she wasn't receiving enough attention from me, she threw herself at my occasional guests, running out with them into the hall when they left.

A Monday morning in August my mother called. She had

gone to the hospital earlier than usual that morning, and Dad had waited for her arrival. As she reached his bed he sought her hand, and with his weary, pain-laden eyes he gazed at her. His love for her had begun over thirty years ago, and he could not leave without once more seeing her. But the pain this last time was more real than his desire to stay with her. Death offered him relief, and he accepted.

As Mom and I entered the room I paused to read the notes attached to the floral arrangements, lamenting the fate of these lovely flowers, clipped and solemnly arranged to represent years of friendship and now sorrow. Their burden was heavy.

He lay in his Sunday suit, the navy blue, with an unfashionably narrow striped tie.

"He never liked his Bloomingdale's ties, did he?" I smiled at Mom.

"He loved them, dear. That's why he kept them in his drawer. He used to like looking at them."

I couldn't remember when I first deliberately chose to love him. I had been his favorite in many ways, perhaps because he saw himself in me. I was quiet and independent as he was, especially before he met Mom. We were both stubborn and proud. He had always supported my whims. He shared his love for music, art, and antiques with me. And he loved animals.

"Poor Mitchie," I said, "I'll bet he misses Dad. Who'll buy him chicken livers now?"

"And who else would open five different cans of cat food until Mitchie finds one he likes?" Mom asked.

"You probably would," I replied.

The paste-white face was handsome, but austere and loveless. I turned away. Friends appeared, and the room grew lively with conversation. The reunion let me momentarily forget the occasion. Sometimes my eyes would drift back to the casket, and someone, following my glance, would remark how nice he looked. In a gesture of comfort others would speak of his suffering and the relief that followed its termination. Before me flashed the image of my father in his hospital room, eaten away by disease and reminded only by pain and sorrow of the life still in him. A team united in purpose strove to keep him alive, while those who loved him prayed that he would die.

The burial took place on a gloomy Friday morning. It was windy and cold in the openness of the cemetery, the kind of day that Dad had always hated. Mom, Paul, and I waited in the gray drizzle, our feet sinking into the soggy earth. The station wagon arrived, and the men gathered to lift the heavy urn that contained his ashes. It fell to the ground. Mom shuddered and turned away. When they had lowered it into the ground and returned the first pieces of moist earth to their place, we joined hands, the three of us, and said good-bye. The sun, previously hidden by a thick pattern of clouds, broke through for just a moment in our final farewell.

I returned to New York the next afternoon. Siggie sat on the floor, gazing soulfully at me with his golden eyes, waiting for encouragement to come up and sit with me. Daphne was not so respectful. Having known me longer, she knew that she could make her usual demands. Sam and Frederick fought, and Sam wore the evidence of defeat on his tail. Natasha went to the laundry bag, selected a dirty sock, and, meowing as she dragged it through the apartment, deposited it selflessly at my feet. How good life was—full of kindness and instinct, love and dirty socks.

I had two days before returning to work. I had two days to feel intensely, to remember lovingly. Two days to share the things that he had loved, and then to let go. The love would remain, expressing itself daily in the living beings who shared my life. Once I returned to work, the habits and demands of my daily life would dominate. There would be no shared memories, for no one here knew him. No one here noticed that he was gone.

In September I registered at Hunter College for a microbiology course. I had graduated from Hunter with a major in English and had continued my studies in graduate school. When I started working in oncology as a research associate, I found my interest drawn to the sciences. My mother reminded me that as a child I worked on my brother's science projects. She interpreted my enthusiasm retrospectively as an early inclination for the field. I think that I enjoyed the challenge of solving a problem, but even more, I think that I wanted to please my big brother.

In school I had avoided elective science courses. It was not until I had worked at the center for two or three years that I recognized my need for and developing interest in science.

I had become familiar with the drugs and dosages, learning for which diseases particular drugs were most effective. I could recognize symptoms and anticipate problems in treatment. When the oncology service did its hospital rounds, I was included. I listened as they discussed each case. I learned what they suspected from the clinical history and symptoms, which tests they requested to establish a diagnosis, and what the diagnosis meant in terms of the animal's life. And then I read about each disease, possible treatments, complications due to treatment. I read about similar diseases and therapy in humans. I subscribed to medical and oncology journals. I read with an understanding based solely on my still limited clinical experience.

But I had reached a point in my scientific career where I needed basic background information. I was trying to master advanced concepts without having learned the fundamentals. So I decided to return to undergraduate study at night. I had no particular goal in mind, except to learn as much as possible about my new field. Each semester I enrolled in one of the courses that I had avoided in my previous academic career. I began with biology.

The microbiology course that I registered for now met once a week on Monday, my day off. It involved a two-hour lecture with a three-hour lab. I enjoyed studying and especially looked forward to the weekly lab.

Lab was my opportunity to understand what I had studied and memorized in lecture. I wanted to learn so that I could apply this knowledge to my work. I could study for exams, I could perfect my laboratory technique, but the true value of my studying became apparent when I understood something at work because of my efforts. When I read an article and it referred to some test that I had performed in lab, I felt that I was making progress.

Chapter 9

With work and school the fall weeks passed quickly. In late October I somehow exposed my cats to an upper respiratory tract virus. Natasha, Daphne, and Siggie remained healthy, but Sam and Frederick became quite ill. Upper respiratory infections (URI) are highly contagious among cats. They are airborne viruses and do not depend upon direct cat-to-cat contact. Even though I was careful about washing my hands after handling a sick cat, I probably brought the virus home on my clothes.

Sneezing, runny noses, red, weepy eyes. Frederick's nose was so congested that he had to breathe through his mouth. They couldn't smell food and wouldn't eat on their own. I didn't want to expose the ward cats, so I kept the two boys, who finally had something in common, home. Sam responded quickly to treatment and soon began to eat on his own. Frederick had a more severe case. He felt miserable, but he was a wonderful patient. I fed him, gave him fluids to prevent dehydration, ointment for his eyes, and antibiotics in case of a secondary bacterial infection. For days we fought to keep him stable, to prevent him from getting weaker. It was a joyous day when he licked baby food off my finger. We had reached the turning point. I went to work feeling optimistic for the first time in two weeks.

Clinic started early, and I had little time to think about my private patient. I felt almost light-headed from lack of worry.

When I walked into the office, Audrey was talking about a new patient.

"She wants to euthanize him, but it's her husband's cat, and he's away on business."

"Who's that, Audrey?" I asked.

"The cat's name is Rasputin. I told her we'd try to help him while she gets in touch with the husband, but the cat's really in bad shape. Wait till you see him."

"Leukemia test positive?" I asked.

"Yes, and pale as a ghost. I think we'll put him in a cage, and I'd like you to put in a catheter for his blood transfusion, if you don't mind. I'll help hold him."

"Do you think he can wait until you're free?"

"Well, he's waited this long, and I don't want him struggling with anyone else."

I carried the young black and white cat to his cage. He cried as though in pain, but he was so weak that he couldn't move. I called Audrey and asked her if I could give him an intravenous drug used for treatment of shock while he waited for his blood. She agreed that it might make him feel better. He let me insert the needle without a struggle, and remained quiet while I gave the drug slowly. I thought he was going to die any moment.

As soon as Audrey was free, I inserted the catheter into his jugular vein and we took our blood samples for the lab. He was lying still in his cage when she left, receiving the blood transfusion. I sat next to him and put my finger on the whitened pads of his right front paw. His nails curled around my finger. I wanted him to know that someone was there. As he lay there he urinated on the cardboard pad, and didn't have the strength to move from that spot. I lifted him and changed the pad. When I left, he still had not moved.

"Well, at least we've done all that we can," I remarked to Audrey on our way out of the building.

"Now it's up to him," she replied. "Did he seem more comfortable?"

"He stopped that plaintive meowing, so he may feel better."

Thursday afternoon, two days after he arrived, I read a notation in Rasputin's record that he was depressed. When I opened the cage door, however, to sit with him, he immediately came and sat on my lap.

"Well, Rasputin, have you figured out what happened to that one day in your life? I think you lost it, and we almost lost you."

He was purring and rolling, slipping off my lap and climbing back on. I was stroking his sparkling white tummy, and he was gazing at me with dreamy, faraway eyes. Siggie eyes, I call them.

"You didn't think life was so good that day, did you? And now look at you. The days just aren't long enough for all the catching up you want to do."

Finally he decided he was hungry again and climbed down from my lap to eat. I changed his litter pan and looked for Audrey.

"Audrey, you have to look at Rasputin." I told her about his progress.

"That is a pretty remarkable response," she agreed. "But how long will it last?"

"I know, until he needs another transfusion, and another," I conceded. His prognosis was grim, and ultimately he would have to be euthanized.

That afternoon was the last time I saw Rasputin. He was euthanized late that day at his owners' request. When I came in the next morning I took a plate of food and my coffee for our morning routine. When I got to his cage, the door was open, the cage empty.

I was glad that Rasputin had at least had two days of happiness with us. I was relieved that he would not suffer again. I would not see him grow gradually thinner and weaker. The memory of our days together is precious. We had grown so close, and I know that he trusted me. I would have been there at the end, had I known. I wanted his last moments to be with a friend, not some doctor he didn't know. I wanted him to be with someone who loved him.

I have seen cats receive multiple blood transfusions over a period of months. The initial interval might be as long as two months, but the period between transfusions almost always shortened until two-week intervals were too long. The effect of the first transfusion was frequently dramatic but diminished with repeated treatments. The cat and the owner accepted a gradually declining life-style as each blood transfusion proved to be less effective than the previous one.

I remember a cat who had been dramatically revived twice over a six-month period. Blood and steroids had rescued him and restored him to a comfortable life. His third crisis occurred during the three-hour period that he was left alone one day. He had been active that morning, eating a normal breakfast. When his owner left for a few hours, he was sleeping comfortably on his chair. When she returned, he was dead. I have always felt that he chose his time deliberately. She had saved him twice by rushing him to the hospital. This third time he convinced his owner that he was fine and died where he wanted to be, in his home.

One owner brought his cat in for several transfusions over a period of months. The cat's condition was slowly worsening when she was admitted for another transfusion. The owner was away, and a friend left her in the hospital after her treatment. For three days she ate well, responded to affection, and seemed comfortable. The owner was returning at the end of the week. On the fourth day the cat's condition was rapidly deteriorating, and we continued supporting her while we awaited word from her owner. We wanted to recommend euthanasia.

As long as the cat was eating I felt that she had some desire to live. When she refused food on the fourth day, she had reached a turning point. Despite our support she did not respond. She seemed to withdraw more each day that I sat with her. On the sixth day she raised herself slowly from the mat and walked to the front of the cage, where I was sitting. She lay down with her head resting on my hand. At the time I thought that she might be feeling stronger, but the next morning when I found her dead in her cage I realized that she had been saying good-bye.

It is a very special area in which I work. So many of the patients that we see are granted a limited amount of time. I know in advance how little time there is to love them and to make them comfortable. Their lives are even more valuable to me, because they must feel when they die that they are loved.

The following Tuesday morning I was late, and Chico convinced me that he hadn't eaten yet. As I put his plate on the floor Audrey walked in.

"I fed him this morning," she said.

"Chico swears that you forgot."

"Chico's mistaken."

"He sees it as a matter of interpretation," I explained.

"He always does when he's wrong," she replied.

He had finished and jumped on her desk. He faced her and boldly stared at her.

"Crazy cat," she muttered, reaching out to pat his neck. He nipped her and sprang from the desk and out of the office just as Jay was coming in.

"How's Frederick doing, Sam?"

"Great. He's trying to make up for all the meals he missed. He even made the mistake of trying to eat Siggie's dinner!" I smiled thinking of gentle Siggie who would share almost anything—a chair, the bed, even me. But not his dinner.

"He's a pretty tough cat," Jay observed. "How about the monster?" he asked as Chico peered around the corner.

"He's doing so well that I hate to treat him," Audrey said. "Yet I'm afraid not to."

"What do you mean?"

"We just don't seem to touch them with the drugs, once the mass comes back."

"But we have had successes with less frequent therapy," Jay replied.

"I just don't want to take any chances with Chico."

There were cats who received treatment every three weeks

and were free of disease. We had extended the interval between treatments for different reasons in each case, and none of them had developed any problems yet. But Chico was still our longest survivor. We had first met him fourteen months ago.

It was exciting when an animal lived beyond our average projected time. But it also raised new questions. We had no precedent to follow in these cases, and we couldn't refer to human medicine without allowing for adjustments. A cat's life expectancy is sixteen to twenty-five years, and because of a cat's size we had to be constantly learning from our exceptional patients; we didn't wish to learn at their expense.

We decided to continue Chico's weekly treatments.

Linda, my cat-sitter, worked on the second floor. One Tuesday in November she called and asked if I could help her with an anemic cat in her ward. The cat needed a jugular catheter for a blood transfusion. Linda was concerned that the cat would be stressed by too much restraint. We called on one another periodically with problem cats because we had similar techniques for holding them. If the cat could be distracted for a moment, the procedure went quickly. Linda had originated the "mouse in the house" story, and now we had a number of episodes. We found that talking softly to the cat was an effective technique in gaining his attention and holding him still. I went down to help, and we set up the transfusion to drip slowly.

"Spotty cat's counting the days until Thanksgiving," she remarked. He was her orange-and-white tiger cat.

"Kentucky Fried Chicken?"

"No, no. My aunt makes a special Spotty cat bag with choice turkey cuts!" she explained.

"Boneless, I presume."

"Oh, yes. She likes the Spot."

I went back upstairs to catch up on some of the work that I had neglected that afternoon. As I sat in the office I thought I heard Chico meowing, but I couldn't find him either in the office or in the hall. He sounded close, then more distant. Finally I couldn't hear him at all.

Audrey and Greg had left for the day, and I went down to the cafeteria to get some coffee. As I got off on the fourth floor there was a group gathered in front of the other elevator.

"What's going on?" I asked.

"There's a cat stuck on top of the elevator. The trapdoor was open and he must have jumped up there."

I had a terrible feeling that I had found Chico.

"Can they reach him?"

"Every time they try to get him, he hisses and moves back."

I worked my way to the front and stepped into the elevator. Mr. Stinson looked down at me from the chair that supported him.

"Oh, no," he greeted me, "don't tell me that's Chico up there."

"It's a distinct possibility, Mr. Stinson. May I take a look?"

I stood on the chair but was unable to reach the trapdoor in the ceiling. I braced myself against the wall with my feet on his back while Mr. Stinson lifted me to the top of the elevator. I shone the flashlight into the darkness.

"Chico," I cooed, "is that you, Chico?"

"Merow," he replied.

"Whatcha doing, Chico?" I asked, trying to remain calm. He was coming toward me.

"Can you grab him?"

"Almost. Come a little closer, angel, I'm not mad."

71

"She's not mad!" I heard muttered from below. Poor Mr. Stinson's back must have been hurting by now. I reached for Chico, and he had time to escape my clumsy grasp, but I think he was tired of the game and wanted to go home. We walked out to applause, but I really thought that Mr. Stinson deserved most of the credit.

One Friday evening in early December as I took the garbage out to the back of my apartment building I heard meowing. Finally I located the source, a gray-and-black feline sorting through the local garbage cans. She was curious but not trustful. She approached me but would not let me pet her. I ran upstairs to bring her some food. She devoured it and gratefully let me pet her. Then she sprang over the fence and disappeared into the darkness.

When I came home from work the next day, I checked the backyard to see if I could spot her in the daylight. There was no sign of her. Thinking she might be a night cat, I decided to look for her again later.

Our Saturday evening routine at home involved reading through the thick sections of the Sunday *Times*. Natasha liked to sleep on the unread pile, allowing me to interrupt her nap as I removed one section at a time. Daphne preferred to crawl between the pages, attacking anything that moved above her tunnel. Siggie disposed of the sections I was done with, shredding them in Clancy style. Sam and Frederick didn't participate but sat on opposite sides of the room, staring at one another until they both closed their eyes in sleep.

That Saturday night I took some food with me when I went out for the Sunday paper. Not seeing her, I left it in the same place. It was a muggy evening with thunder sounding in the distance. The *Times* was late that night, and as I waited the clouds fulfilled their promise, and it began to rain. Back in my apartment I found a cardboard box and carried it downstairs for my new waif. She was eating the soggy food, and meowed when she saw me. She sat in the shelter I provided until I moved to bring her food over to her. She followed me. Food in the box, she again stepped in, and I stood up to go inside. It was pouring. She meowed. She followed me. I showed her the box, she rubbed against my leg.

I ran upstairs to find the cat carrier, and my cats disappeared when they saw it. I returned to find her in the box. She ran to greet me. The thunder was roaring, creeping closer and closer. I took her to the AMC, vaccinated her, fed her, and, promising I would find her a good home, left her sleeping in the ward.

By Tuesday she had discarded her gray mackintosh and had become a shiny white-and-black cat. Her name, I decided, was Sadie.

As Christmas approached I worked on developing my seasonal spirit. It was impossible not to remember the events of the previous year. This year was Christmas without Clancy.

Clinic was over, and I was turning out the lights on our Christmas tree when the operator paged me.

"Samantha, it's Monica Cosgrove. I'm calling you because I brought my cat in last night, and—"

"Mykonos?" I interrupted.

"No, Adam," she explained. "He got ill suddenly, and I can't get through to the doctor until phone time—I was wondering if you'd check on him for me."

"Of course," I assured her. "Is he in Intensive Care?"

"Yes, they were quite concerned about him last night."

73

"Do you know what's wrong?" I asked.

"They thought it was his heart," she replied. "He's never been sick before, and now, all of a sudden—"

"Let me check, and I'll call you back."

I looked for a large black Persian. Not finding him, I checked the list of transfers and, finally, deaths. Cosgrove. I found the doctor in charge of the case, and he was just calling Monica to inform her. I decided to wait.

Back in our waiting room I admired the tree. This year we had tried to make Christmas special for our clients by making a tree of dried white branches and multicolored lights. The only ornaments were silhouettes that I had made using construction paper. Each client wrote his pet's name on an ornament and placed it on the tree. I made one for Clancy. I enjoyed watching more ornaments added each day. Chico. Oliver. Tabby Rodolitz. She came in for her yearly checkup, and since she was still climbing trees, even with three legs, we put her ornament near the top of the tree, close to Clancy's.

I spoke to Monica Cosgrove a few days later and told her about Sadie. She was such a special cat that I was particular about placing her. But I was also aware of the difficulty of finding a home for a full-grown cat. Kittens were easier to place. But Monica didn't hesitate. She didn't even want to see her first before deciding. She arrived with a carrier to take Sadie home. Sadie looked immaculate the day that Monica came to pick her up. I placed her in the red-and-black carrier and tried not to hear her plaintive meows as she was carried off. She had come a long way from the street; now she was moving to Fifth Avenue. She would be happy. Monica selected a white ornament for Mykonos, a black and white for Sadie, and added them to our tree.

I made giant catnip mice for some of our patients. For the three weeks before Christmas my cats at home rolled and stretched, wallowing in stolen catnip. While I was cutting material and sewing, Daphne invaded the storehouse of feline ambrosia, carrying it from room to room on her feet for everyone to share. Euphoria became their norm.

On Christmas Eve I surprised them with even more catnip mice, but the novelty was wearing off. Siggie got a windup mouse which he loved and hated. Hearing it clatter across the hardwood floor, he raced from the far end of the apartment to immobilize it by pouncing on it. Then, enraged by the still spinning rubber tail, Siggie seized it in his mouth and shook its body. Finally, when I revived it one time too many, he hid it.

Natasha swallowed a piece of tinsel which miraculously passed through her without doing damage. We eliminated tinsel henceforth from our decorations.

Everyone assumed his place on the bed Christmas Eve night. We were warm, secure, and healthy. I closed my eyes contentedly and fell asleep.

Christmas morning was the time we exchanged presents when our family was together in Buffalo. As Christmas Eve was special for me, so was Christmas Day a time of memories for Mom. This was her first Christmas without Dad. She had arranged a busy schedule, visiting and dining with friends, so I called her early in the morning.

"Do you have snow?" I asked.

"There's plenty on the ground," she replied, "and more falling now. I wish you were here to see it."

I planned to work the next day, shortening the holiday as

much as possible this year. My final exam was in the first week in January, so I used my free time to study. I had mailed Mom's present and card. And I called. My brother was with his wife's family, and he had called Mom too. But she was alone. I had placed my own needs before hers. She had wanted to be home, and she had not insisted on my visit. But she was alone, and I should have been there.

Oliver Cromwell Smith had come in the week before Christmas because the Smiths had noticed a change in his behavior. He was still eating well but he was grouchy at times, and this was abnormal for mellow Oliver. We had run blood tests on him to give us some indication of physical abnormalities, but all the tests were normal. We thought it was a warning signal, but all we could do was watch him and wait. Now, three weeks later, Mrs. Smith was back.

"He hasn't eaten well the past few days," she began. I stroked him as he sat on the exam table. "And he's quite touchy, not at all himself."

As she spoke he hissed and began growling softly. I don't think I had ever seen him hiss before.

"Well," began Dr. Hayes after a cursory exam, "his kidneys are very large and irregular."

"But could this happen so suddenly?"

"I think he was telling us three weeks ago, but it was too early to detect then."

"What do you think it is, Dr. Hayes?"

"I'm afraid he has lymphosarcoma in his kidneys. But let's take him into the hospital, get some more blood tests, X rays, and get him started on fluid therapy."

"Lymphosarcoma? Isn't that what Clancy had?" Mrs. Smith directed this question at me.

"Yes," I replied, remembering how much alike they were

"We should have the results back this afternoon, and then we'll talk about our next step."

"Will he stay up here?" she asked, again looking at me.

I smiled. "Of course we'll keep him with us. He's family."

"But he's not himself. He's so grouchy these days, poor Oliver."

"All the more like family, then. We usually see his best side. He's allowed to be grouchy when he's not feeling well."

Oliver stayed in H Ward. An aspiration biopsy of his kidney confirmed the diagnosis of lymphosarcoma. We kept him on fluid therapy to regulate his kidney function and began treating his disease. Three days later he was affectionate and eating well. He was ready to go home.

I thought of Clancy often during those days when Oliver stayed with us. I was sad and angry about Oliver, for he had been one of my mainstays, a reminder that some of our long-term patients resisted disease. For nine years he had remained normal, and we had shared three of those happy years. He had resisted longer than Clancy, but now even he had succumbed. As he grew stronger I did too, although I worried because Clancy was still so vivid in my memory. I did not share these fears, these feelings with anyone. There seemed to be no answer.

Chapter 10

My new year began in January when a new ward cat entered my life.

She came to stay for such a little while, sneaking into my life and hiding, barely noticed, in the shadow of my recognition. I cannot say what day I brought her out to wander, or even why, except that her shyness spoke to me. So tiny, so frightened, so slow to adjust to the status of caged feline. I don't even remember how or when I found her again. I do recall she disappeared, hiding in some unknown place, one of the places that would soon become so familiar to us both.

Her becoming a part of my life happened so naturally that I was not paying attention. And then, all of a sudden, my day began when I looked in her cage and she meowed and ran to the front. No longer in my shadow, but my shadow itself, she waited patiently while I finished treatments, and then pranced beside me, through the waiting room, into the office.

On clinic days she sat by the door, watching the patients as they arrived. Unlike Clancy she was a spectator. She would observe until someone noticed her, and then she would seek cover. Occasional trips to the elevator, escorting me to the ladies' room, and then she sought a private place and slept contently. She chose the drawer, sometimes the windowsill or cabinet, and, often, her basket.

She blossomed in these months. Although still timid, she would venture into the clinic area, visiting patients, entering and exiting the booths under the partition until she found me. Her name was Fledermaus, because she was batlike with her harelip and a small groove down the center of her flattened nose.

She came into my life during a time of isolation for me. The needs of the oncology group did not converge, and our purposes met only with the patient. We communicated on this level alone.

Jay had left for a new position at Cornell. He had been a central figure in the unit. His surgical schedule linked him with the rest of the hospital, whereas we sometimes felt isolated on the eighth floor. He also seemed to link together our own diversified unit. We were all very different people, people who would probably not have found one another in any other aspect of life. Our interest in cancer and our mutual concern for our patients bound us and in some ways kept us apart from the rest of the hospital. With Jay gone, the separation seemed more painful.

I missed him already. I had depended upon him, trusting his judgment about all our patients, including Siggie. I had depended upon him emotionally too. Although we rarely spoke of feelings, we both seemed to accept their reality and to respect the silence that often controlled and sustained them.

We had worked together in clinic that morning of his last day, and then he was scheduled for surgery. We both pretended that it was just another day. When I left the building that afternoon, I knew that I would not see him again. But saying good-bye was too final. It dispelled all other possibilities. Instead I wrote him a letter, and the next day when I came in I found a note from him.

Each member of our unit tried to set aside the conflicts and problems, the anticipations and disappointments, involved in daily living. After all, our attitudes and decisions affected other lives. The patient must always come first and must always receive our complete attention. Our first obligation was to the patient, but our responsibility extended to the owner.

How could the client who came to us for help know what had already touched our lives that morning, what burden any one of us carried? It was not a question of relative importance, of whose burden was heavier. His cat's illness was the most important thing in his life, and his cat's well-being must be equally important to us.

When a pet is sick, there is an ever-present weight that burdens us throughout the day. Sometimes we are not even consciously aware of it until it is lifted, like a persistent headache that becomes a part of our normal sensations. Only when the pain is alleviated are we aware of how unpleasant it was.

With my work at the hospital sometimes it seemed that the pain of illness persisted, differing only in the object of my concern. I tried to maintain the separation between home and work, but if one of my family was sick my concern became an inseparable part of me. One week I arrived at work for three consecutive days to find that a patient had died unexpectedly. At home I watched my cats, watched them eat, groom one another, and sleep. I watched them breathing in slumber, and fell asleep with my hand over Daphne's heart.

It must have been equally difficult for the other members of our unit. They all had their own pets at home, and when they were ill, it must have seemed as though there was no relief.

My own needs seemed altered now. It was as though I existed only in terms of my function; that what I was, what I was not, and my feelings about the gap between were nonexistent.

Home and work no longer balanced one another. The fine line that I had drawn seemed now to divide my life into two distinct areas. When I was home, I wanted to remain there. At home I felt comfortable and needed. Some mornings I dreaded going to work. It was the animals who drew me out of the apartment and to the center. I went reluctantly, fearing disappointment or failure.

Only Fledermaus, first in shy curiosity, walked upon the cold surface of my frozen emotions, leaving gentle paw prints on the glassy panel. Deliberately and lovingly my quiet friend filled me with such longing for the world outside me that I opened up the window to touch her. As the roots of plants must thaw in early spring, so did my senses tingle and reawaken. My vision focused through her eyes, and joy manifested itself in her vital impulses.

I had found a friend in the outside world who trusted and loved me. Someone who chose me deliberately, accepted me completely. Someone who needed me. I had found a friend who waited for me to choose the time, who did not force me to take action or to speak, who did not try to alter my life so that she might find her role more easily. She simply loved me and trusted me. And I, in my inability to reach out, to communicate my sense of loss, my fears, my disappointments, I needed this tiny, six-pound Fledermaus.

She constantly delighted me. I would open a drawer and there she was inside. Standing in an exam room with a client, I would feel her brush against my leg or see her tail and hind legs as she squeezed herself back under the partition if she found a dog in the room.

Greg called me into his office one Tuesday morning, and the Maus trailed timidly behind me. I sat in the chair by the open door and she positioned herself opposite me with the way to escape in view. She eyed Greg warily as she inched her way toward me.

"I tried to get some blood from Fledermaus yesterday," he confessed. At the sound of her name she froze. "Duerrel held her, and she got upset, so he let her go. We couldn't catch her after that."

I smiled at my little six-pound terror. "How much do you need?" I asked.

"About twelve milliliters," he replied.

"We'll discuss it and get back to you," I said, getting up to leave. Fledermaus pranced ahead.

Donating blood periodically was one of Fledermaus's responsibilities as a resident of H Ward. She was a leukemia test positive normal cat who was donated from a large household of cats. We did not use her blood for transfusions, but as a control to determine whether a laboratory test was working properly. When she first arrived, she had to be tranquilized before we could obtain even small amounts of blood. Now, however, we had reached an understanding. She would stay still if I held her while another person took the sample. But we were both impatient: only one attempt was endured.

As she grew bolder she often slept in the cardboard box where we kept our small syringes for use during clinic. They were packaged to ensure sterility. We would gently pull out a syringe at a time, like jackstraws, so as not to interrupt her sleep. But as soon as Greg walked in the clinic she flew, batlike, across the room and into her drawer. He no longer asked me to put her in her cage, and he could not catch her.

We grew together, Fledermaus and I, both of us becoming stronger and more secure; more dependent upon one another. And on those gray afternoons when darkness crept up on us early, my friend and I would sit in the empty waiting room and watch the rain in its animated descent. Occasionally the Maus would walk across the windowsill to sharpen her claws on the bark supporting the leafy green philodendron. From our eighth-story fortress we could see the glistening raindrops on the Fifty-ninth Street Bridge, and the river dark and frigid beneath us. The day was over, but we still had tomorrow.

Chico in his tall, lean wildness was not jealous of the Maus. I think he missed Jay, especially on weekends. Audrey had not taken any weekend trips, so Chico was confined to the center. But he was secure in his habitat, and didn't have much time to devote to me. He was too busy with life, exhausting each day with deliberation.

The spring semester at Hunter began in February, and I registered for another lecture and lab. The lecture in cell biology was held two nights a week: I arranged to take the lab again on Monday. I studied some afternoons with the Maus curled up in my lap, or I studied at home with Daphne lying on my book and Siggie shredding my notes. Only Natasha encouraged my scholastic pursuits by respectfully sleeping on the bed.

I was accustomed to the usual distractions at home. Sam and Frederick would serenade me from the kitchen. Their song was a low-pitched monotone that was a five-minute warning prelude to battle. By stamping my feet and calling their names from the room in which I studied, I could deter the impending fight without putting down my pencil.

I was unaccustomed to sharing the apartment with a guest. Mary and I had met in the restaurant business. Before I came to the center, I had worked at Friday's, a local restaurant where I continued to work on Sundays. Mary had worked as waitress, hostess, and assistant manager in various restaurants. She was an artist and often left her job to paint. Over the years I saw her off to Woodstock, Martha's Vineyard, Paris and India. In late March, Mary called me from Kennedy Airport. She had just returned after two years in Paris. Our last communication had been at Christmas, and she had not mentioned coming home.

"I can't wait to see you," I said.

"I'll be there in less than an hour."

Mary arrived with two suitcases and moved into the front room. We carried the mattress into the living room, and Mary slept there on the floor. I used the boxspring in the bedroom.

Mary wanted to visit our friends at the restaurant, so we celebrated her return by going out. A week later Mary was still celebrating, having left me at home after the second long night. Some nights I was studying when she came home early, around 10 P.M. She crawled under the covers on the mattress, slept an hour, and went out again.

The cats scattered when she came through the apartment. The heels of her shoes clattered against the wood floor, and she walked swiftly. Only Daphne accepted Mary as a challenge rather than a threat. Daphne ran a few steps ahead of Mary and then stopped suddenly. Mary inevitably tripped, and Daphne disappeared under the bed.

Mary had a wonderful raspy voice. Her speech was sporadic and full of frequent emotional spurts during which her voice rose almost an octave. When she was happy, upset or surprised, she screamed, and when she screamed, the cats disappeared. Sam sometimes stayed with her on the mattress, but only when he was sure that she was sleeping. Daphne ran back and forth over her body nightly as though Mary were an obstacle on Daphne's sprint course.

Some mornings when I left for work, I found Mary's keys still in the apartment door. It was easy to get angry at Mary, but it was difficult to remain angry.

One afternoon in April I came home from work, and no one met me at the door. Mary was usually home in the afternoon, but I was more surprised that the cats didn't meet me. None of them. The apartment was silent.

I walked slowly through the rooms to the living room, sensing that something was wrong. When I reached the front room, I saw Mary lying on the mattress. The floor-to-ceiling cat tree was lying next to her on the floor. I stood there for a moment, just staring at her. I didn't see any blood.

"Mary," I whispered. "Mary?"

At that moment Daphne ran up the back of the armchair, onto the cushion, and pounced, landing on Mary's back. Mary screamed and started laughing. Daphne disappeared into the carpeted compartment of the newly positioned cat tree.

I never heard the story of how the tree fell, but since it has never fallen again, I tend to think that Mary was involved. She seized the opportunity to play a little joke on me, but Daphne had the last laugh. Fortunately no one was hurt, and the other cats gradually became visible again. Except Siggie. Poor Siggie was afraid that if he moved, something else might happen, so I had to coax him out from under my bed.

Mary and I finally stopped laughing, and we decided that she needed a job. In May, Mary moved uptown, and I began studying for my final exam at the end of the month.

When school was over Mary called to tell me that she had a cat. I had never encouraged Mary to adopt a pet because I didn't think she wanted the responsibility. Sometimes Mary left town on a few hours' notice, and a cat might impede her spontaneity. I knew that Mary would never mistreat an animal, but I wondered if someone who left her keys in the door and then spent hours searching for them could remember to feed the cat and change the litter.

On my way to meet her new roommate I pictured a robust male who sat boldly on the kitchen table at dinnertime. I imagined a cat who yawned and resumed his nap when awakened by Mary's outbursts, a cat agile and solid enough to avoid being attacked by Mary's lethal heels.

I sat with Mary for three hours before I saw a ball of fur flash by me. Tiffany was a delicate, long-haired female who sought cover at the sound of a sneeze. But they worked it out somehow, and Tiffany never missed a meal. She slept on Mary's bed, and only rarely walked across one of Mary's watercolors.

Chapter 11

The days were getting warmer when Audrey and I again took Chico overnight to Fire Island. The same client had invited us to use her summer place. This time we drove with Chico after work on Saturday. It was warm in the car, and Chico kept throwing himself against the sides of the carrier, so I attached the leash to his collar and allowed him to explore until the fifth time that he attempted to sit on the accelerator. Thereafter he was confined to the back seat.

He paced, sliding from side to side as Audrey changed lanes. When she slowed down for the tollbooth he slipped off the seat. I put the open carrier on the seat and eventually he settled down, but he wasn't happy until we were on the ferry to the island.

The weather forecast for Sunday promised a sunny beach day. I was planning on taking calculus in summer school this year, and this excursion would probably have to carry me through the summer. Classes met four nights a week, and weekends would be reserved for studying. I was looking forward to lying on an uncrowded beach for the entire day.

We picked up some food in town before we went out to the house. Chico was hungry and, after eating, fell asleep on the living room couch while we watched TV. Audrey went to bed, and I fell asleep on the sofa. During the night Chico sat up, stretched, and jumped down to join Audrey in her room. I turned off the TV.

The morning after we arrived I was in the kitchen making coffee when I heard Audrey scream.

"Samantha!" she shrieked.

I ran into her bedroom and found her leaning out a now screenless window.

"He's gone," she began. "I saw it happening, and I just couldn't believe it. Chico's gone."

The house was surrounded by thick woods. I grabbed some roast beef and we went out to begin our search. Bushes, trees, overgrown grass. How would we ever find him?

As though reading my thoughts, Audrey questioned me. "What can we do? We can't go back without him. Should I call Greg? I can't call Greg and tell him we lost Chico. What will we do, Samantha?"

Greg had warned us about losing Chico on one of our excursions. He warned us, not because he thought that we were careless, but because he knew that Chico was crafty.

"We'll keep looking. He's here somewhere, Audrey."

She laughed.

I don't know how long we searched, how long he sat quietly and watched our increasing anxiety, but Chico's enjoyment always involved participation. He was not a spectator. Finally he allowed Audrey to spot him, but he was not ready to be captured yet. He sat where we could not reach him, protected by undergrowth and thorny bushes, waiting for the incentive to emerge. I unwrapped the roast beef. He accepted the reward.

The sun was bright and warm, inviting us to the beach, but Chico could not be trusted. The house was too hot with all the windows and doors closed, and we would probably worry about him all day anyway. We took the next ferry back to the mainland.

As clinic was ending one Thursday in late June, I went down to Radiology to retrieve Chico. We repeated his X rays routinely about every three months. They were normal again.

"That's a strange cat you sent us," one of the new technicians remarked.

"Who, Chico?" I asked innocently.

"He doesn't seem to think he's a cat," he observed.

"Well, Chico's usually right, but we don't know what else to call him," I explained.

I left Chico in the office and was walking through the waiting room when I was greeted by the Maus.

"She was looking for you," Mrs. Firpo remarked. Her cat, Stripes, was reclining in his carrier. I was delighted to see him. He had stayed in the hospital with us two years ago while we diagnosed his leukemia and began treatment. He was accustomed to having things done his way, and once he let us know that, we readily accepted his suggestions. His way was usually easier and better anyway.

By giving him small amounts of blood from a leukemia-immune cat every two weeks, we had been able to achieve remission for almost two years. We had tried this therapy on many other cats without getting the same response. Stripes was in many ways a special cat.

"We hardly see you anymore," I remarked. "Now that you're feeling better you don't need us, right?"

"He's doing so well, Sam. Every three weeks now, and he's never sick at home. Look how much weight he's gained."

"If I didn't know better, I might think that was fat." I smiled, looking at the marbled tiger in the open carrier. He rolled on his back. "No, I can see it's all muscle!"

"She looks real good," Mrs. Firpo remarked, slowly reaching to pet Fledermaus on my lap. She was instinctively good with cats, and the Maus didn't move. "She's getting better with people."

"Well, not all people," I replied, feeling her tense as Greg called Mrs. Firpo into the booth. We both laughed. "We're going to the Playboy Club this weekend, with Audrey."

"I didn't know they allowed pets."

"I don't think they do."

It was a warm July afternoon. By the time clinic was over and our hospital cases stabilized, we had missed the intense heat of the sun. Audrey and I packed the car for the short drive to New Jersey. I had worked Friday night at the restaurant, so that I could have Sunday off. I didn't often do this, because the switch meant working until 4 A.M. Saturday morning.

Fledermaus was sitting in her basket, unaware of the forthcoming adventure. Once in the car, however, she lost her nonchalance.

Sharp, piercing cries issued from the wicker basket. The

Maus rarely meowed, but when she did it took the form of a squeak. I took her out, and she attempted to escape under the seat. She would not be pacified, and panted in the heat. I had brought a facecloth and sponged her coat to keep her cool. Finally she settled down in her basket.

"She's more comfortable now, I think," I told Audrey, who was concentrating on the city traffic. "She likes the highways better than the New York City streets."

"I don't blame her. Between the cabs and the potholes there's not much room for relaxation."

It was a ninety-minute drive to New Jersey's Vernon Valley and Great Gorge. The air was turning cooler, and the roads were getting hillier as we approached the Playboy Club.

"How do you think we should handle this?" I asked Audrey, for she had stayed at the club often during ski season. "Are you sure they don't allow pets?"

"No, but they might be a little suspicious if we ask now."

"True," I replied, "and this is more challenging anyway."

"Well, she's quiet now. Let's just hope she decides to stay that way."

"Do we both have to go through the lobby?"

"I think we'll park the car first, and then I'll go register, get the key, and come back to the car for you."

"That sounds good. That way I'll have time to get her out from under the seat."

"She didn't!"

"Just now."

We turned into the grounds and followed a few cars to the arrival area. The people ahead of us got out of their cars, and an attendant drove off in the first car.

"Valet parking!" Audrey cried. "They never had valet parking. We have to unload here."

"Do we have a choice?"

"Samantha, he's unloading the cars. Where is she?"

"I've got my hand on her, but where is he?"

Just then the door opened and the doorman began taking the luggage out.

"Oh, I'll carry that," I explained, grabbing with my free hand for the wicker basket.

"Hello, it's nice to see you again. You haven't been here since last winter, have you?" He had recognized Audrey, and she steered him away from the car as I fumbled for the Maus. She had stretched herself out so that she could not get out the same way that she had entered. Her head was up, her back arched, her legs rigid. Finally out and into the basket. We entered the lobby.

"MOW!" screeched my little basket. I looked around with everyone else, trying to locate the source of the cry.

"Audrey, I think I'll go sit in that secluded little lounge while you register." She had already deserted me after the first *mow*, and I shuffled off to the lounge.

We sat in the dark shadows of the lounge. To strangers I was a figure huddled over a wicker basket, speaking to myself in low, continuous tones. Audrey returned with the key. The bellhop had gone on ahead, and we began the long walk to the room. We spoke loudly through the corridors and shopping area, bursting into hysterical laughter when the Maus squeaked. She increased her volume; we increased ours. The porter was waiting at the elevator, and while Audrey explained my claustrophobia I headed for the stairs with my basket.

I watched from the stairwell as the bellhop walked down the corridor back toward the elevator. I knocked on the door.

"He couldn't understand what had happened to you, why

you didn't meet us here. So I told him you had to take the stairs slowly. Heart, you know."

"He must think I'm a delight to travel with!"

Fledermaus scurried out of the basket and under the bed. Her shyness lasted about two hours. We unpacked our bags and watched a tennis match on TV. I found a Maus ball and rolled it by the bed. No response. Again and again I rolled the ball, more intrigued with this game than the one on television. Finally I changed my tactics and rolled the ball directly at my partner under the bed. She returned it. Shortly thereafter Fledermaus emerged from her cave.

The maid called at the door, and the Maus ran to greet her. We turned down the extra towels. I was tired, having worked the night before, and we decided to share dinner in our room with Fledermaus. She was very anxious to meet the room service waiter who delivered our food. Knowing how much she enjoyed our trips to the ladies' room at the center, I coaxed her into the bathroom when he arrived.

Delightful Maus! She seemed to adapt well to the change in her routine. What a new joy this was for us. We would sit on my bed and watch television or nap—things that we had never shared before. I lifted the sheet and coaxed her under. Unhappy Maus! She must have felt trapped, because she escaped and hid under the bed. For another hour I pleaded with her to trust me again. She gave me another chance, purring beside me on the bed. But I remember most walking into the room and seeing her there by the door, waiting. She couldn't sit still, she was so filled with delight, with herself, with us, with the moment. I do not know how she spent her time alone. Sleeping, I imagine, for she was so full of energy and vitality whenever I discovered her again, that it was too intense to maintain.

Summer school began the Tuesday after July 4. We drove back to the city in time for my first class.

We returned to work on Wednesday that week. When Audrey came in, both Chico and Fledermaus were eating.

"I think we should have taken Chico with us," Audrey commented.

"We couldn't take both of them, Audrey, and it was the Maus's first adventure outside the hospital."

"I know, but Chico likes me better."

"Fledermaus likes you. She's just shy, you know that. It took her a long time to begin to trust me. She's not at all like Chico."

"I know. He likes me."

I knew that Audrey's feelings were hurt when the Maus ran from her. I also knew that Audrey was aware of Fledermaus's painful timidity, and that she didn't really take this as a personal rejection. Truthfully, however, she did prefer Chico's company. I compromised.

"Next time will be his turn."

He was walking toward Audrey's desk, presumably for a nap during clinic.

"Don't forget your treatment today, Chico," she reminded him. He left the room.

I walked into the waiting room and knew that it would be a nice day. Mrs. Smith and Oliver were there.

"He's doing real well, Samantha," Mrs. Smith began.

"Shouldn't he be in Maine?"

"We got a late start this year, but I'll be staying longer at the end of the summer, so he won't mind," she explained.

Greg examined Oliver while I sat next to him on the table and petted him.

"His kidneys feel good," Greg commented when he finished the exam. "They're small and only the right one feels a little irregular. Let's go ahead and treat him."

"Yes," I agreed. "He still has some packing to do for his trip. And you'll need medication for the summer, right?"

We treated him, and he held on to the edge of the table with his front paws as we injected a hind leg. He neither growled nor hissed. He was feeling good. As Greg called the next client into the booth I wrote out Oliver's treatment schedule for his Maine doctor.

"Sam, you have to meet this cat," Greg remarked, entering the office after his initial exam. "His spleen is enlarged, and the referring veterinarian reports a high white blood cell count. The cat has diarrhea, and he's losing weight. Let's get a CBC, differential, and a check for mast cells."

The presence of this particular type of cell would confirm a diagnosis of mast-cell tumor, distinguishing the cat's illness from leukemia. The symptoms could be similar.

"Do we have a leukemia virus on him?" I asked.

"Negative, but let's repeat it."

"Are we hospitalizing him?"

"No. That's why I want you to meet him. He's seventeen" —Greg smiled—"and his name is Sam."

Sam was a marmalade-and-white tiger cat. His face was white with orange contrast beginning with a distinct stripe at the outside corner of each eye. His nose seemed as wide as Siggie's was long. His eyes, set wide apart, were shades of green with gold-and-rust flecks. He was tall and long, and had obviously been a much larger cat before his illness. The odor of diarrhea was evident, but Sam was still fastidious about grooming himself. What a noble old gentleman. He resisted

95

any restraint, so I merely lifted his chin, and Greg took the blood sample from Sam's jugular vein.

The blood tests indicated that Sam had leukemia. He returned to clinic for a bone marrow aspiration, which confirmed the diagnosis of chronic lymphocytic leukemia.

Sam's leukemia was a type that we rarely see in cats. It was unrelated to the disease that is called feline leukemia, because it was not caused by a virus, and it was not contagious. He was still in good shape despite his weight loss. He never stopped eating; in fact his appetite was voracious. We started him on chemotherapy that was given in pill form at home. The medication took a long time to work, but within a few months we saw a dramatic response in his blood count. He seemed even stronger and he continued to eat well. His diarrhea was slowly lessening.

I think that my favorite stage of cathood is old age. Kittens are exhilarating, exhausting balls of energy. Not easily intimidated, they torment large dogs and attack the toes of giant human beings. Unmannerly creatures, they ask no respect and give none in return. The first meal, the first trip to the litter box, the first toy—all are joyful moments of satisfaction for an owner.

The years are full of first experiences with a cat. Each new home, each added piece of furniture, each new guest introduced to the household, all are moments savored and magnified by the curious feline.

But it is the older cat who intrigues me—the cat who has established his preferences, who growls when his routine is interrupted; the cat who walks up to his favorite chair and stares at the younger feline occupant until she moves. The cat who has been there through the years, who knows every one of his owner's moods. He who has earned his owner's respect and has become a valued friend and companion. Sam was such a cat.

His owner traveled extensively. When he was out of town, his housekeeper cared for the other three cats. Sam needed medication, however, so a close friend of his went to the apartment daily to treat Sam and to make sure he was doing well. Ed was also involved in business with Sam's owner. When they were both out of town, Sam stayed at the hospital. I let him out as much as possible, but he was terribly unhappy in his cage and meowed pitifully when I left him at night.

The last night of Sam's second hospital stay Ed called me from California to tell me that their plane had been delayed. They would arrive in New York around midnight and wanted to pick up Sam then. I was anxious for Sam to go home too, so we arranged for them to pick up Sam at my apartment, since animals could not be released from the hospital after 9:30 P.M.

I brought Sam home with me that night. I had never brought a patient home and none of my friends' cats visited. I was afraid of exposing my cats to one of the many contagious feline disorders, ranging from the leukemia virus or upper respiratory tract viruses to ringworm or even fleas. Sam was an exception. His illness was not contagious, and his age compelled me to bend one of my rules.

At eleven the phone rang, and Ed informed me that the flight had been delayed again. Sam was sitting by the window, methodically destroying my plants. He ate. After marching through the apartment, he returned to the window, a prime location. My other cats ignored him, except Daphne, who followed him everywhere. When I took an hour's nap at 3 A.M., Sam joined me on the bed. Only Natasha assumed her rightful place at my feet.

At 4:30 A.M. Ed rang my buzzer, and Sam went home. From that time Sam stayed at our place when they went out of town.

Chico was due for his treatment when clinic was over. It was a humid July afternoon. I sat and watched him as he returned to the office after receiving his injection.

"Audrey, look how he's walking. He's staggering," I said as he moved across the room. Just then he attempted to spring to the counter above him and fell back to the floor. That from a cat who rarely missed his mark.

"I think he's having a reaction," Audrey said, walking over to him.

Chico was bewildered by the fall, and perhaps slightly embarrassed. He *mff*ed as Audrey tried to examine him and ran away. But a few minutes later he seemed fine again.

"Maybe it's time to spread out his treatments, Audrey," I suggested, knowing that we had discussed this previously. "It's almost two years."

"Well, we know from his X rays that he's in remission," she conceded. "Let's go to every other week for a while."

Satisfied with this decision, Chico trotted out of the office carrying his catnip mouse in his mouth.

"I wonder if his whiskers will grow back," I commented. One of the long-term effects of chemotherapy on cats was that their whiskers broke off close to their muzzles. The therapy did not cause any other hair loss, but it did alter the texture of the cats' fur. Their coats became softer, like an undercoat.

Chico was still a magnificent-looking cat. His cropped whiskers accentuated his aristocratic nose and golden, almond-shaped eyes. His body was plump and extremely huggable if he allowed himself to be caught. Chico wandered back into the office, now mouseless. As he strolled past my chair I seized the unsuspecting feline, turning him toward me. Anticipating a kiss, he held my face at paw's length.

The summer passed quickly, probably because my nights and weekends were overwhelmed by calculus. I used to enjoy math. Like biology, math, I felt, was logical. The concepts, if initially difficult, were ultimately comprehensible. I don't think I ever understood calculus. I attended every class, completed the homework, took the exams, and did well in the course. But I never understood calculus.

In mid-August the course ended and I felt that I had accomplished something, although I was not certain what it was. I was just so pleased to spend my evenings at home without feeling compelled to study. I brushed the cats, clipped their nails, and cleaned their ears. Natasha helped by grooming Daphne and Siggie. Frederick and Sam groomed themselves.

Natasha and Daphne were cordial to one another, but they were not friends. Before I worked at the hospital, Natasha had been my only cat. I thought that she would enjoy some companionship. A friend of mine was trying to find homes for a litter of kittens. I told him to choose the one who looked like a Daphne.

Daphne is black and white with a round, flat face. A black mask covers her eyes and rises to a point high on her forehead. She has a white ruff encircling her neck. Her chest and four legs are white, her tail black. She looks like a Daphne.

Natasha accepted her into our home, grooming her and patiently sharing all her possessions. Sometimes after a particularly trying day with the kitten Natasha would come and sit with me, as in the old days. She allowed Daphne to sit on the arm of the chair, or even next to us on the cushion, but when Daphne tried to crowd her out of her rightful place, Natasha swatted her.

As each cat entered our household Natasha made concessions. She shared the bed, she groomed the growing Siggie cat. But when Natasha walked across the living room to my chair, all cats deferred to her. We respected Natasha.

Loyal, accepting, through every day, through my every mood, Natasha was my friend. She was always there.

We were peaceful and content at home, enjoying uneventful days. The calm had spread to the center, and for a while my most important decision was what to feed the Maus and Chico.

Chico seemed to adjust well to the longer intervals between treatments. In late August, however, we noticed that he was slightly icteric—there was a yellow tinge to his membrane coloring. We took blood for a biochemical analysis and discovered that his liver was not functioning normally.

"All right, what do we do now?" Audrey asked as she looked at the results of the blood test. "I'm sure these abnormalities are a result of our treatment."

"Well, if he were a client's cat," I replied, "you would recommend hospitalizing him, and you'd start him on fluids. Since he's not eating as well, you would supplement him with potassium and some B vitamins."

"But that means a jugular catheter and cage confinement."

"But only for a few days, probably."

"That's true. If he responds, he'll be out again shortly. As it is, I wonder how much he's enjoying his freedom anyway."

With more awareness and regret than anyone, perhaps,

Audrey chose to support Chico in confinement for a few days in order to strengthen him for his forthcoming reprieve. The subsequent blood tests confirmed that his condition had improved.

Thursday morning I entered the ward to begin the treatments. Chico was dead in his cage. It was not the death that any of us would have wanted for this untamed domestic cat who had shared two years of his life with us, for he had died alone and confined.

But his three days of confinement were far outweighed by his weekends with Jay and his trips to Fire Island. Chico had demanded the best of all that we could give him. I don't think that he was disappointed.

Chapter 12

It was Labor Day weekend. I had taken the next day off, and when I arrived at work the Maus would not eat.

"Fleder's angry with me," I told Audrey as I pulled a chair over to her desk.

"She may be angry, but she's not letting you out of her sight. I think she's sulking."

"Did she eat yesterday?" I asked.

"I really don't know, Samantha. We didn't have her out. I know Duerrel fed her, but I'm not sure if she ate."

"Poor Maus, Aunt Audrey didn't let you out," I teased.

"Aunt Audrey can't catch her to put her back at night," Audrey retorted. The phone on her desk rang, and Audrey answered it as Fledermaus jumped onto my lap. She only stayed a moment and sprang back to the floor.

"Audrey," I interrupted, pointing to my white lab coat, now spotted with blood.

She was smiling as she hung up the phone. "She's been trying to tell you since you came in!" Audrey exclaimed.

Fledermaus was an unspayed female, and she had developed an infected uterus. The treatment was surgery.

"No wonder she wouldn't eat," I reasoned. "She knew she needed to be spayed today."

"Smart cat—I'll call down and schedule her."

"Fledermaus is having surgery?" Greg asked, overhearing the arrangements as he walked in.

"Dr. Fledermaus," I replied.

While the Maus was in surgery I tried to find other things to do to keep me out of the surgery area. I checked my mail and found a postcard from the Smiths. Oliver Cromwell and his family were enjoying Maine. They would be back in the city soon.

How many more summers, I wondered, could we give Oliver? His life was normal now, and we were grateful for this extension. The extension, however, would not be indefinite. We rarely spoke about the inevitable outcome, but Mrs. Smith must have wondered some evenings as she sat on the porch overlooking the ocean—with Oliver in her lap.

Fledermaus was still groggy when I brought her upstairs after her surgery. I wanted to sit and hold her for a while, but she was coming out of the anesthesia and insisted upon crawling on the floor. I put her in her cage to limit her exertions, and then stayed and watched her for a long time before I went home.

By the next morning the Maus was active and hungry. She pranced ahead of me into the office, eager to resume her daily habits, beginning with breakfast. She was shy about her tiny incision and allowed only me to look at it. But by Saturday clinic her confidence was restored, and she reclaimed control of the office. A week later she was completely healed and her fur was growing back. She remained visible until clinic became hectic, around eleven, at which time she retired.

Saturday is usually our busiest clinic day. We see only rechecks, and sometimes as many as thirty-five patients. This morning was typical, with several feline mammary tumor patients. Some of the cats and their owners were old friends.

Monica Cosgrove brought in both Mykonos, our regular visitor, and Sadie.

"They both look wonderful, Monica," I remarked. "Are they getting along?"

"Well, if Mykonos gives in, they do!" she replied.

"Strong-willed female!" I whispered to Sadie as I rubbed her ear.

"I'm having some friends over for an open house next Sunday. Can you come? I'd like you to see these two in their natural environment."

"I'd love to," I replied, "as long as you've cleared it with Sadie!"

I walked into the office as Fledermaus was emerging from the drawer.

"She's up," Audrey announced.

"Dr. Fledermaus, you're missing clinic," I advised her politely.

"I think she's shy about her sutures and haircut," Audrey suggested.

"Maybe she wants to specialize. You know, consult on the more interesting cases?"

"Don't we all?" replied Audrey, walking in to see her next patient.

Later, when clinic was over and our hospital cases cared for, I decided to remove the Maus's sutures.

"She's healed beautifully," I commented to Audrey, who had observed the ritual.

"So where are you going on vacation?" she asked.

"I don't even know yet. I can't decide about Fledermaus. I don't want to go without h but I'm afraid to take her with me."

"You mean the stress of the trip? I would think there's a certain amount of stress involved in her missing you."

"Not to mention my stress in worrying about her while I'm gone!"

In our clinical experience we have learned to consider the effects of a wide range of events, physical and emotional, which we group together and label stress. We try to maintain a status quo with our feline leukemia virus positive patients. In Fledermaus's case an infected uterus was dangerous, not only because it was the site of a severe infection, but because the uterus itself could rupture. Frequently after a procedure such as a spay we have encountered recovery problems or sometimes the development of a virus-related disease.

Fledermaus jumped on my lap and curled up for a short nap after her late-afternoon snack.

"Well, Maus, should we aim for the quality or quantity of our days?"

"What does she say?" asked Audrey.

"She wants both."

I still had time to decide on our destination, so I promised the Maus that I'd bring Sunday morning coffee and the Travel Section from the *Times* the next morning.

* * *

I really didn't know much about Monica Cosgrove, I realized, as I walked to her apartment Sunday night.

My relationship with the clients in our clinic is special and focused. Our immediate common ground is our feeling about animals. Since I take care of the cats when they are hospitalized, I have an emotional attachment to them and a glimpse of the qualities that make each cat unique. Their owners and I have an immediate intimacy, and yet we know little about one another.

Generally our relationships are initiated by and dependent upon clinic visits. I will see clients and their pets weekly or biweekly for months, and then treatment intervals will be extended, or the local veterinarian administers treatments. Or, in some cases, our patient dies.

It is a joyous moment for all of us when a client returns to our clinic with a new pet. Kitten or full-grown cat, we know it has found a wonderful home. Sometimes the new pet looks amazingly similar to the one who died, and sometimes there is no physical resemblance at all. Occasionally we see glimpses of the same temperament or hauntingly familiar mannerisms.

Of all the relationships that I have enjoyed through our clinic only a few have extended into my life outside the hospital. A few friendships begun at the clinic have slowly grown over months and sometimes years into relationships that touched other aspects of my life. Beth was one of these.

Over a five-year period Beth had lost seven cats, all feline leukemia test positive. She had taken in some of our positive cats from the hospital when two of her original three cats died. Knowing the uncertain prognosis for these cats, she had adopted them to share whatever time they had. Finally when her seventh cat, her favorite and the one she had brought to our clinic originally, died, we talked about her next adoption. Beth was willing to continue, but we talked about starting a family of healthy, normal cats. There was no guarantee that a new pet would escape illness or tragedy, but Beth's chances would be the average chances that we accept when we have pets. Lots of healthy, normal cats needed homes too.

She adopted four at once: a kitten whose inexperienced mom had chewed one of his feet; a tough, young, street-wise tom; one of our spry female blood-donor cats; and an elegant chestnut Oriental shorthair.

We have stayed in touch throughout the more common feline episodes of parasites, vaccinations, and ear mites. We had shared the difficult times first, years ago, and we were beginning to share some good times now.

Monica too had reached out to include me in another part of her life. It was a lovely gesture, and I was looking forward to it.

Most of Monica's guests that Sunday were in their late forties, but there were a few younger people present. Monica introduced me to a group of her contemporaries, and I listened as they reminisced about school days. It was then that I learned that she had been a registered nurse at one time.

Monica introduced me as Mykonos's nurse, explaining where I worked and in which department. One person in the group asked, "Isn't it sad working with dying animals?"

I smiled at Monica as I replied. "Our patients are not all dying animals. Look at Mykonos."

"But all that experimentation—" she continued.

I interrupted. "We're a treatment center," I attempted to explain. "Our patients are pets who are diagnosed as having disease. We never inflict disease." I could feel my tone changing from that of conversation to lecture. "I enjoy working with our patients," I concluded.

"It's not at all like you're imagining," Monica interjected. But her guest had the last word as she turned away.

"I still think it's depressing," she murmured.

Monica lived in a lovely old townhouse off Fifth Avenue. Her apartment was charming. The hall from the kitchen to the bedroom was tiled in black and white. Sadie sat in the corridor as though she were aware of the striking effect she created. Mykonos sprawled on the sofa between two guests. We sat in comfortable overstuffed chairs in an airy white living room. I admired Monica's paintings, some of them done by friends, and the lovely Oriental carpet in the center of the room. It was a warm and tasteful home. Monica had chosen her belongings carefully.

I had wondered how the cats would respond to my presence in their home. I worried that Sadie might think that I had come to take her back to the hospital, or Mykonos that I had come to treat him. But they felt secure in their home, and they greeted me cordially. Sadie even saw me to the elevator when I left.

One of Monica's friends, Margaret, left at the same time, and we walked together for a couple of blocks. She and Monica had been friends for many years. I thought that Monica probably worked at her relationships, keeping them active. She enjoyed bringing people together, hoping that those she cared about would like one another. I felt that I knew Monica a little better, and I liked her.

On my walk home, after leaving Margaret, I thought again about my vacation and the Maus. I decided on mid-September, and somewhere near the ocean. My first choice was

Maine, but the trip would be long and difficult with my companion. There would be one plane ride, on a flight that allowed her to travel in the cabin with me.

I found a hotel that welcomed pets, and so on a brisk and overcast day Fledermaus and I discovered Hyannis.

Chapter 13

We left the Animal Medical Center early in the morning. Fledermaus traveled in her regulation airline carrier. We arrived at the Marine Terminal, and I let the Maus out of the carrier with her harness and leash. She screamed to every passenger in the terminal that I was abducting her. Finally she settled down in her open box, but she was not happy. Our plane left at 9:20 A.M.

It was a small plane and takeoff was noisy. The carrier was under the seat, and I leaned over with my fingers in the openings of the cat box to let her know that I was near. She had remained silent from the moment we entered the plane. Once in the air I hurried to open the carrier, anxious about the noise from takeoff, and the silence of the Maus. She looked at me with round saucer eyes, her body melting into the shape of my hand. I held the open carrier in my lap for the entire trip. The stewardess was very understanding.

At 10:50 we arrived at Hyannis and took a cab to our motel. We were across the street from the bay. Our room was not ready, but I introduced the Maus and the management welcomed her. We went for coffee and milk at the coffee shop.

Our room was clean and compact, with two windows: one overlooking the grassy area behind the motel, and the other facing the front walkway. I unpacked my suitcase while the Maus inspected her new surroundings, especially the area under the bed. I unpacked my books and piled them on the round table by the rear window.

Fall semester evening courses at Hunter had begun the week after Labor Day. I had registered for two courses, physics and chemistry, and prepared myself to suffer throughout their duration. I had started thinking of an advanced degree when I realized how much I enjoyed biology, but the advanced biology courses also required a chemistry background. My schedule included four nights at Hunter, with my chemistry lab lasting until 10 P.M. This week school was closed for three days, so I was only missing one lecture.

The town center was a ten-minute walk. I put a Do Not Disturb sign on the door so that the Maus would not be interrupted, and set out to inspect the stores. After window-shopping for a while, I found the supermarket, selected some cat food and litter for my friend, and returned home.

I climbed the steps to the walkway outside our room and saw Fledermaus standing on the chair, peeking through the loosely closed curtains. I tapped on the window, and she jumped down to meet me at the door. Each time I returned she greeted me this way.

Early fall at the Cape is a solitary time. The air is crisp and full of promises of something still more wonderful. And when the sun is teasing through the pattern of clouds above, a breeze, a mere breeze, summons all its strength and exhausts itself in a moment.

My shadow and I let this breeze take us with it, following its path through the unmown grass. We welcomed the solitude and took our place within it. Fledermaus resented the harness and leash, but we were close to the road, and I couldn't risk losing her. Fledermaus spotted a huge oak tree and ran to inspect it. Stretching on her hind legs, she scratched the bark sharply. Perhaps she thought it was a giant philodendron.

It was a strange experience to work with a cat for so many months and then to live with her for the first time. As well as I thought I knew the Maus, I had no idea of her preferences or habits. I made drawers into beds for her, left her traveling box open, and watched to see where she would sleep. She chose my suede handbag on the bed, and she remained there at least until I dozed, for in the mornings I found her sleeping under the bed.

I rented a bicycle to force myself to tour the Cape. I almost resented the sunny days when I felt obliged to sit outside by the empty pool. I wanted to read, I had to study, and I wanted the Maus with me.

On one of my bicycle jaunts I found a sportswear outlet that sold wonderfully colored T-shirts. The backgrounds came in bright green, blue, yellow, and bold purple. On the front of the shirt was a fat smiling Cheshire cat. I bought some in each color.

On another outing I discovered a bookstore with rooms of old dusty books, some on shelves, some piled in stacks on the floor. I spent hours sorting through them, touching the worn bindings, turning the soft, fragile pages. The books were randomly stacked, and I examined them methodically, hoping to discover a forgotten first edition of a favorite author.

Riding back to the motel, I stopped to buy more toys for the Maus. She always thanked me by playing with a new mouse or ball. Under the bed she stored all the discarded, used toys. The management very nicely informed me that she was also hiding other things under the bed. The Maus wasn't used to litter at the center, and although she used the box most of the time, apparently she did not always use it. The area was cleaned, and she never missed the box again.

I think we both preferred the gray and dreary days when I would lie upon the bed, sipping coffee and reading. We listened to music, and she would lie beside me as we waited for the rain. When I went out to get our dinner, she seemed content to sleep but always waited for me at the door when I came home. We shared the first impressions of fall that mid-September in Hyannis, for when we returned to New York, the weather was just beginning to grow cool.

"Welcome back," Audrey greeted us as I dropped Fledermaus off at the AMC. The Maus immediately checked all her favorite spots to make sure that nothing had changed and that no one new had moved in. I put some food down, and she ate.

"She looks like she's gained weight. I guess the trip agreed with her. Tell me all about it."

The trip was still too fresh in my mind. I was reluctant to talk about it, as though words would make it somehow less real to me.

"Well, it was a low-keyed vacation. Lots of reading, listening, and thinking. And excellent company. The Cape is beautiful. I rented a bike and did some cycling."

"Sam, how was your trip?" Greg asked as he came into the office. "Dr. Fledermaus looks great."

She had just finished her dinner and was cleaning herself. I went over and sat on the floor next to her, and occasionally she licked my hand as I petted her.

"Anything new here?" I asked.

"Nothing really, except that we missed you guys—both of you."

"Well, we missed you too, but I think we needed to slow down our lives, at least for a little while. Are you ready to speed things up, Maus?" I asked. In reply she settled into her basket for a nap. I checked my friends in the ward and then hurried home to feed my family. Linda had taken care of them. They all looked well fed and healthy, but they had missed me, and I was glad to see them.

I immediately resumed my intense study schedule, having failed in my good intentions to study on vacation. Natasha didn't even bother to wait up for me anymore. Siggie was confused by my late hours. He would wake up at three in the morning, jump off the bed, and sit by my desk chair until I assured him that I was okay. Some nights I studied through the entire night, just as I had in my early college days. In those days we studied before an exam, usually because we hadn't opened a book until that long night. Now it was different.

Physics and chemistry didn't apply directly to my work, as biology did, but they offered a different challenge. Both courses required constant work at problem-solving. Every night I worked on pages of problems, stopping only to arbitrate an argument between Sam and Frederick or to play with Daphne. She loved having a playmate at these unusual hours. When she was ready, she jumped on the desk and grabbed at my pencil until she won my complete attention.

The problems required a long time to penetrate. They were challenging because they involved translating words into numbers. During the first week of my physics course, I couldn't even fill a page with attempted solutions. The professor taught us how to translate the words into a diagram and then how to use the numbers to set up an equation. I felt myself learning, and I was excited by each new accomplishment.

The first weeks back at the clinic were hectic as I tried to catch up and get ahead of the work I had missed. But soon the routine became familiar again, and it seemed like a long time ago that Maus and I had been away. The air was turning cooler, and I was already believing in the first snowfall.

Early in October Fledermaus was not eating as well as usual. She seemed quieter and more withdrawn. We checked some blood tests and they were normal. She did not have a fever, and we couldn't find anything specifically wrong.

Then, on Friday, October 13, I watched her as she sat on the windowsill. She was breathing heavily. Radiographs confirmed that she had an anterior mediastinal mass, a mass located above her heart. We treated her with chemotherapy immediately, and I put her back in her cage for the night. She was exhausted and confused by the day's ordeal, and she did not object to her confinement.

That night and many nights thereafter I tried to understand what had happened. Had I accelerated her illness, or caused it, by taking her with me? Was the trip too stressful for her? On the other hand, how would I feel if I had not taken her and this had happened? Frustration finally led me to accept the realization that my guilt or innocence could not help me. *Why* didn't really matter anymore.

Fledermaus went into remission and seemed more comfortable at first. She still spent her days and nights in the office and participated in daily clinics. There were days when she seemed almost her old self. She did better with minimal therapy, and the less intensive treatment schedule still kept her in remission.

But her appetite was waning, and she was losing weight. Her coat was not the shiny, sleek fur that she proudly groomed. She no longer pranced beside me wherever I went, but now walked slowly, knowing that I would wait. She slept more, content to let me hold her. She was often alone. Tired and depressed, even her purr was softer and less frequent.

I loved her so. Some days I would come home from work, exhausted physically and emotionally. I just wanted to forget every obligation that I had assumed. I wanted this time at home to be a time in itself, not just an interlude before I had to return to the hospital or go to class or study for my courses. Natasha seemed to understand that my quiet moments at home included her. She sat peacefully on my lap, purring gently.

Sometimes Beth would call, or Jesse, another friend from the clinic. His cat had mammary gland tumors and was receiving immunotherapy every two weeks. He always managed to make me laugh, often unintentionally. Beth and Jesse could distract me with wonderful cat stories. Jesse's other cat, a Siamese, cawed and chirped each time he saw the Goodyear Blimp outside the window. Beth's three-and-a-half-legged cat was fast outgrowing kittenhood in size, becoming a sleek, athletic feline. Daphne often ended our conversations abruptly by stepping on the telephone and disconnecting us.

My afternoons at home connected me with other lives. By the time I returned to my chair, Natasha had left for the bed and Frederick sprawled uncompromisingly on the cushion. The mood was broken, and it was time to return to my studies. Often I took a textbook with me when I returned to the hospital to visit Fledermaus.

Each day, including weekends, I sat and coaxed her to eat, sometimes force-feeding her. I talked to her of winter and snow, of Christmas, and of how we would wait together. I spoke of how I needed her, of how she had slowed my pace and taught me to stop and see, to touch, to share my muted presence when a presence was all I had. And all the while I thought the times were limitless, that I could always come again and rest beside my friend.

She was improving, until she suffered yet another setback on a Tuesday late in November. Radiographs revealed pneumonia. She continued to grow weaker.

Wednesday night I sat with her for a few hours, and she ate a little on her own. She was so weak that she walked to the litter box, but did not have the strength to crawl back. But it wasn't cancer that was making her so weak, I kept reminding myself. If she could just get stronger. I sat and read with my hand beside her tiny body.

When I first walked into the office Thursday morning I couldn't find her. I looked in all her favorite places, although she had not frequented them recently. When I saw her in the bucket with the cleaning supplies, I laughed—how like my Maus. But when I lifted her out, she was so weak that she just lay on the chair, Audrey's chair. I tried to feed her, but the food just stayed on her mouth. And her eyes pleaded with me to stop. I cleaned her tiny, delicate face, her funny nose, and stroked her as she lay on her side. She had given up. And then, as I held her, she died without a sound or movement.

She had loved me enough to wait for me, but she had decided, when I could not, that life was not worthy of her suffering. She was ready, but I was not, for I had not used all that time that she was ill to prepare myself. It was as though I thought that I could bring her through this crisis because I loved and needed her so. But in my love and need I forgot to look at her—this tiny, delicate creature who depended upon me. I wanted to help her, to make her live. I was not ready, but she could wait no longer.

Fledermaus died on Thanksgiving Day. It was raining.

Each day brought with it a new pain. The awareness that something is different. The stillness you hear as you enter the room. The realization that there is now total privacy in the bathroom. The first snowfall of the year—how could I have known that when it finally arrived my little bat would be gone? That I would view the Christmas tree without one ornament amiss, the presents in order? No dishevelled box with shredded tissue paper in which that knowing cat compactly squeezed the finest of all gifts, herself. The long and painful time of firsts without her.

I spoke with a friend whose cat had died about the loneliness of mourning. I wondered about our clients who come in faithfully, week after week, sometimes for years. What happens to them once their pet dies? And what happens to their grief? At least while they are at our clinic they are surrounded by other people facing similar problems. Sometimes we can tell them what to expect in terms of signs, and we can begin to go through the painful process of death and loss with them. But death ends the process abruptly, and they are left to seek their own consolation.

Whenever a patient is brought in to be euthanized in our clinic, we try to see the client immediately to spare him the endless, painful wait. He has already endured enough before he walked into the exam room with his pet. He has placed his cat in the carrier that morning, knowing that this would be the last time. He has made the trip that they made together for weeks or months or years. And then, once in the exam room, he says the words, those difficult, final words that he has known and held in until now.

The client can stay or wait outside the room until the injection has been administered. It is an individual choice. Some clients want to be there and feel that their pet needs them there. For them it is the final gesture in their relationship. Others feel that their distress will make it more difficult for the animal.

The walk from the exam room, through the crowded clinic, where other clients are waiting with their pets, to the elevator, and out of the building must be a long, lonely walk. I remember a client who stayed with his frightened Siamese when we gave her the injection of euthanasia solution. He stayed with her alone for a few minutes, and then picked up her empty blue carrier and left for work. He used to take her to the office after her weekly treatment, and his co-workers always fussed over her. What a painful moment it must have been for him when the first person who saw her carrier by his desk asked how she was.

Sometimes there is a moment to talk before the client leaves, but more often he is struggling to maintain his composure, and nothing is said.

When a person dies the loss is acknowledged in mourning, funerals, and condolences. The bereaved is accepted as a person who suffers a loss of companionship and love. With an animal, however, the feelings of sorrow and loss are not shared. I remember a doctor at the hospital asking me one day, about a week before Fleder died, what was so special about that cat. "She's only a little black cat," he said. As though there were millions, or even one, just like her.

One evening my mother called, and while we talked she asked me how my little black cat was doing. I tried to answer but could not. After a long pause she asked, "When did it happen?"

"Thanksgiving morning," I replied.

"I'm so sorry, dear. But you had such a nice vacation together, and she had a good life with you."

But it was not enough.

"And you have your others."

But it was not the same.

Christmas demanded attention, and though it came upon me too suddenly this year, I began making preparations. Denying my cat family the yearly adventure of setting up the tree would not help me. It was not their loss. The clients and our patients deserved the special attention of Christmas too. The white branched tree, now a tradition, appeared in the clinic. The first ornaments were Clancy, Chico, and Fledermaus.

I was planning on going home to Buffalo to spend a few days with my mother before Christmas. She was going to spend the holiday with Paul and his family. The last time that Mom had needed me I had sent a present instead. A gift was a painless but inadequate substitute for oneself. This time I would go myself. Linda and Carol were available for my cats.

As Mom and I watched the snow falling silently outside the living room window we talked. We talked about my brother Paul, about the weather, the health food store she owned. We talked about friendship.

I grew up in a family that believed in friendship. Mom's best friend was my godmother, and she and Mom had gone through high school together. My godmother lived in the next block and came to dinner every Friday for as long as I can remember. She and Dad worked at County Hall, downtown, and traveled to and from work together. Friday dinner conversation centered on the week's work, and Paul, Mom, and I were entertained by personal incidents and insights. Mom enjoyed the friendship between the two of them as if it were a part of her.

I learned how special, how rare such a relationship was. As a child I always had one close friend. As I grew older I made friends slowly, being social with a number of people but often not having one special friend. I learned, sometimes by making mistakes, to let friendship evolve.

When called upon to be a friend I learned to consider what friendship meant to me. What qualities were important to me, what limits I placed for my own integrity.

I felt that it was an important relationship. It was a relationship that involved sharing, but it also insisted upon individual rights. It was not a partnership like marriage. It was not the union of two people for one common purpose. Instead it involved a selective sharing. The sharing would grow as the trust in one another grew. An offered trust, a sharing of emotion, was never a friend's right to demand; it was a gift given to someone worthy of honoring it. As a gift it should not be appraised or judged or passed on to others, as one's own to give. The feelings and confidences shared with a true friend were the finest example of faith in that relationship. I believed in honoring that trust. But sharing could not be rushed by either person. Imposing one's own timing on a friend was selfish. It was seeing someone else's life only in terms of your own.

In a moment of need a friend was a miracle. Her absence or, even more, her betrayal, was devastating.

I was glad to be there for my mother. Not to make decisions for her or to insist upon the way she live her life. Respecting her judgment, I wanted to be there for her because I cared. I wanted to have the patience and the selflessness to wait for her to confide in me. I wanted to see her pain in terms of her life, not mine. I wanted to be her friend, and I needed her as mine.

Mom and I sat by the fireplace watching Mitchie creep closer and closer to the warmth of the fire. We were changing, both of us growing in our individual lives. But the changes were bringing us closer, enabling us to talk now as independent women, as two people who liked one another.

Slowly the words evolved, first sheltering emotion, and then, with patience, giving emotion form. We talked about past Christmases with Paul and Dad. She told me that one of Dad's old friends had called recently, asking to speak to him.

It seemed so strange to me that for him my father had been alive all this time.

I tried to induce Mitchie to sleep on the couch with me, but he was Mom's cat now and followed her everywhere.

Mom began preparing for her trip out west, and I returned to my cat family for another traditional celebration.

My own feelings had to be dealt with. I had put them aside, knowing that they needed time and attention, and knowing that they would be there when the time was right to bring them forth. I thought that I could face my loss, accept it, and go on, and all this was true. But as with my mother's loss, only time would affect its intensity, only time would finally heal the wound.

Winter seemed to linger long into the new year, as though waiting until the pain and sorrow of the past year had been dispelled. But I was not in tune with nature's plan, and finally spring could wait no longer.

The mornings were clear and cool as I walked down the hill to work. The black cat sat upon his window ledge, awaiting the robin's return as a sure indication that spring was here. Perhaps it was the early hour, perhaps the fragrance of blossoms in the air, or perhaps the magic of spring itself that caused my mind to wander the distance of years in those morning walks. It was as though my mind had lost its sense of time. Images merged in some faint resemblance to a dream: something plucked that grows beyond all time. A glimpse that justifies its truth; a voice that says it never was.

I found my mood determined by the direction of the wind or the colors of the sky. Emotions associated with names and places emerged. Emotions long buried, emotions that time could not touch, nor life sustain. My dreams and recollections blended, and one became no more real than the other. My thoughts, my words, my Fledermaus—which was more real?

My habits, so familiar, remained unchanged. Morning coffee, treatments, clinic. Nothing had changed. Nothing in the world had changed to mark this devastating loss in my life.

And in my need to carry on I lost myself in the daily habits and occurrences of living. Sorrow is its own place, and it was there alone that I felt secure. For outside that refuge her life, her dear life, and that which had made me special were lost forever. Silence ensured my memory, as though words, once shared, would no longer belong to me.

For comfort I turned to those who could not speak; to those who loved and needed me.

Chapter 14

Every afternoon the doctors have a phone time during which they accept calls from clients whose pets are in the hospital, clients who have questions about treatment, reactions, diet, appointments, and new clients. During this period I fed the cats in the ward. Duerrel usually fed them hospital food early in the morning, and the cats always welcomed this afternoon snack. He left me extra cans of the balanced feline diet, and I incorporated that food into a buffet. I tried to add some variety to their diet by using commercial cat food and dry food. I added debittered primary yeast to the canned food.

A few months earlier I had noticed how scruffy some of our residents looked. Their coats were not shiny, and some of them were quite thin. I thought that perhaps they were not getting enough variety in their diets. Some of them had been served the same hospital food for years, and often would not eat it. The yeast would supply them with B vitamins and minerals. Since the B vitamins are water soluble, they would not be stored in the liver but would have to be supplied more frequently. They liked the yeast mixed with their food, and I had noticed an incredible difference in their appearance since I had added it to their diet. Some clients also reported a decrease in flea and skin problems.

I loved this time of day. It gave me a chance to visit with each cat, and it also helped me to detect any problems.

I put some dry food in Evelyn's cage and waited to see if she would eat. Evelyn was a twelve-pound silver tabby who usually devoured everything on her plate. I had mentioned to Audrey the day before that Evelyn was unusually finicky. Today she didn't eat. When phone time was over, Audrey returned to the office.

"Would you look at Evelyn?" I asked her. "She won't eat the dry food, and I think she's breathing abnormally."

"Why don't you see if she'll eat the baby food?" Audrey suggested. "She is breathing too rapidly."

"Her temperature's normal, but she doesn't seem right," I added.

Evelyn ate the baby food, and Audrey and I agreed to get blood tests and X rays on her the next morning.

Friday morning Evelyn was more depressed, and her temperature had fallen to 99°, about one degree below normal. We took her to Radiology and stayed there with her in case she was stressed by the ordeal.

Audrey saw the cardiologist in the hall and called him over to look at Evelyn.

"Larry, she's getting worse every time I look at her. Will you look at her films with us?"

Evelyn was lying in the cage, cold and cyanotic. The film confirmed that she was in congestive heart failure.

"Let's get her to ICU, Sam," Larry said, as he told Audrey what to do. I heard him tell her, "We've never saved one. It happens too quickly, and no matter what we do, we seem to lose them." Turning to go, he saw that I had heard. "But we'll try. Maybe Evelyn will be different."

Larry was the expert in this area, and we waited to see if Evelyn would respond to his treatment. After five days in Intensive Care she still had not eaten anything.

"Thank goodness she has that excess fat to rely on," Audrey commented as we stood by her cage.

"Poor Evelyn," I replied, "food was her only joy, and now she doesn't even have that. It hasn't been much of a life for her, has it?"

"Well, I think she's better off with us than at the other animal shelter where she lived. But you're right, she's always been a blood donor."

"She's helped so many other cats, but she's never had a person of her own to love. I wonder if she has the will to live."

"Even if she does, I don't know if that's enough," Audrey replied.

"Evelyn, if you pull through, I promise you that you'll be the queen of the unit. You can go into retirement and lounge around in the office."

Another week passed while she stayed in Intensive Care. Larry was encouraged.

"She's a pretty tough cat," he remarked to me. "We just lost another one yesterday, but Evelyn seems to be hanging on."

She was magnificent. Finally, after two weeks in ICU,

Evelyn came home to H Ward. We made a special house for her in her cage, and Audrey carried her around every day to view the other cats. Evelyn was growing stronger and her appetite was returning. She was even pouting again.

"Evelyn wants to make sure you haven't forgotten your promise," Audrey mentioned one afternoon.

"Trust me, Evelyn," I replied, "we owe you. I'm just waiting for your doctor's okay."

It was a Wednesday when Evelyn was first allowed in the office. Linda came up to visit shortly before eight. She brought coffee and a jelly doughnut. Evelyn was not shy, and when Linda started eating, Evelyn insisted upon sharing. Thereafter Linda always brought two doughnuts.

Evelyn stayed with us in the office for most of the morning. When the Maine students walked past the office with their lunches, however, Evelyn decided that she could improve her lot. She jumped from the counter to follow them.

At first she divided her time equally between the office and the apartment. In the mornings Evelyn lounged for hours on the windowsill, brazenly stretching her tabby body, exposing each stripe to the sun's warm caress. But the afternoons belonged to the students. She would stay in their living room while they studied or watched the afternoon soaps on TV.

After a few months of this routine Evelyn wanted a change. After breakfast in the office she now swayed down the hall to the bedroom door. She meowed until one of the students let her in, and we did not see her again until late afternoon.

Larry Tilley, her cardiologist, was pleased with her progress and frequently stopped by her cage in the afternoon to visit her.

"Why is she always so grouchy?" he teased. The combination of Evelyn's vertical stripes and the straight horizontal line of her eyes gave the impression that she was always frowning.

"Maybe she doesn't like your prescription for cage rest," I suggested. We all felt that Evelyn's condition was helped by the peaceful life that she was leading. She knew that she was the queen, and she wouldn't let anyone forget it.

A few days later I was in the office after clinic when Audrey walked in.

"Didn't I see Mykonos in clinic today?" I asked. "Why didn't Monica Cosgrove bring him in?"

"I meant to tell you, but then we got so involved in other things. Monica's in the hospital for a biopsy today. She found a lump in her breast. Her friend brought Mykonos in for his treatment, and she left the number at the hospital for you to call."

The next afternoon I called Monica at the hospital.

"How are you feeling?" I began.

"Well, the biopsy was malignant, so I'm a little sore, but fine otherwise," she replied.

"When will you be coming home?"

"Probably in a few days. I'm anxious to get out of here."

"Well, I can understand that. Do you need anything? Is Margaret taking care of the cats, or do you need someone to feed them?"

"No, Margaret's keeping an eye on them. I hear Mykonos checked out well yesterday."

"Yes, he's doing so well. And he's always the perfect gentleman—no fuss, no nonsense!"

"I just hope that I do as well as he did on his chemotherapy. I'm using him as my example to get through this thing."

"You two have been through a lot together. I'm sure he'll do his part."

Exams at Hunter were over and I registered for the spring semester. I continued my chemistry course, but I wanted more biology, so I registered for a course in immunology. Classes began in February.

It was in February that I found a tiny lump on Natasha's mammary gland. I examined all my cats routinely. Handling them and playing with them had somehow developed into an opportunity to check periodically for masses, lymph node enlargement, and, with Sam and Frederick, bite wounds. I checked both girls for mammary gland abnormalities.

Natasha was twelve years old. I had missed her kittenhood, for I adopted her when she was two years old. My closest friend had found her at the Humane Society and took her home as an eight-week-old kitten. For almost two years Carolyn had tried to ignore her cat allergy, and when she decided to return to California, she asked me to take care of Natasha while she was gone.

She was a beautiful calico cat and an excellent roommate. She was reserved and shy at first, but she soon discovered that she could trust me. When Carolyn had called and told me that she was staying in California, I asked her if I could keep Natasha. She agreed.

I waited a few days after first locating the nodule. I was shocked at having found it, and I needed a few days to convince myself that it was real. Now that I had located it, however, it was difficult for me just to pet Natasha without checking to see if it was still there and still the same size. I took her into the clinic to have it checked. It was only two millimeters in diameter. We knew that size was not related to malignancy, but that it was related to prognosis. Both Audrey and Dr. Greene examined her.

Dr. Greene was a fine surgeon who had worked for years at the center. He and Jay were friends, and they respected one another's work. I felt confident about asking Dr. Greene's opinion. I trusted him with my cat.

"I think we should biopsy it, just to make sure," he began.

"I think we should do a radical mastectomy. It's probably malignant, and that way she'd need only one anesthesia," Audrey observed.

"But it might be benign," I said, "and that's extensive surgery for a benign growth."

"You know as well as I do that it's probably not benign," she replied. "I think we've already had our fifteen percent this year."

"Let me look at her more closely when she's under anesthesia and clipped, and we can decide then. We can always send up a frozen section, although they're not that reliable."

I waited outside the surgery area while Dr. Greene performed the radical mastectomy.

Suddenly the lines that I had drawn separating work and home were beginning to merge. My routine examinations had previously been a reassurance. Somehow I never expected to find anything. But seeing Natasha in recovery changed that. My cat had cancer. It had found its way into our refuge.

Natasha recovered beautifully from the anesthesia, and as soon as she was mobile she attempted to chew out her sutures. The collar I put around her neck distressed her more, I think, than the surgery itself. She cried, she staggered, she fell. She growled. Frustration and anger prompted my stoic calico to complain as I have never heard her before. She hurt and she was confused, but I could deal with those feelings and could try to make her more comfortable. For she was alive, and although I had no guarantee that she would live any number of days or months or years, at least I knew that we were giving it our best try. I had decided for her that one day of severe discomfort was a fair price for a better prognosis. Perhaps not tomorrow, but in a few days it would be all right again, and we could go on as before. Experience has taught us the dangerous and rapid course that cancer of the mammary glands in cats takes. When I left she was sleeping on her blanket, exhausted from her battle with the collar. She had lost that one, for her sutures were dry and intact. And the other battle, well, with the other she would have many fighting on her side.

The day after Natasha's surgery I took her home. She still had her Elizabethan collar to keep her from licking her long incision line. My loving feline family hissed and sniffed at her as their welcoming gesture. The collar upset them almost as much as it incapacitated her. Now that she had room and energy to walk she insisted that she could only walk in one direction—backwards. She ate dinner and managed to store most of the food on the collar. We were all distressed. I removed the collar, threatening to replace it if she bothered her sutures. She jumped up on the bed and we watched one another until she fell asleep, purring. In ten days I removed the sutures. She had healed beautifully.

We started Natasha on immunotherapy injections, which I gave her weekly. We both preferred at-home treatments, and I checked her carefully for any new masses. I treated her on my day off, early in the morning. She slept most of the day and occasionally vomited, but she was ready for dinner by late afternoon.

As Natasha resumed her normal life I began to live more comfortably with our new routine. I checked her mammary glands only when I treated her, accepting her activity and appetite as signs of well-being. She was my number-one cat, special because of who she was, not what she had. I couldn't forget her disease, for ignorance and neglect were not in her best interest. But neither were anxiety and overzealousness. I helped her by treating her disease, and she helped me to accept it.

Chapter 15

Mom came to New York for a few days in March. She loved cats, but she was accustomed to a one-cat household. I invited her to stay with us, assuring her that I would understand her preference for hotel accommodations. She had met Daphne and Natasha, but my three males were new to her. She accepted the invitation.

I had told her about Natasha's surgery and therapy. I'm not sure what she expected to see, but she was surprised at how healthy and active Tasha was. Daphne immediately seized the opportunity to demand more attention. She jumped on the bed where Mom was sitting and paraded over her lap. She rubbed against her arm, threw her body against Mom's leg.

"She remembers me," Mom said proudly.

"Are you sure you remember her?" I asked, knowing what Daphne was up to.

"Of course," she replied, putting her hand on Daphne's exposed furry side. Daphne had been waiting. She rolled over, grabbing Mom's hand with her two front paws and simultaneously kicking her wrist and arm with her rabbit back feet. Daphne always got Mom, and Mom always came back for more.

We spent Monday shopping at Bloomingdale's. When we returned home, we opened our packages, and the cats sampled the new boxes and shopping bags. I slept on an air mattress in the living room, and Mom slept on the bed with Frederick and Siggie. Sam was a little shy and, like the polar bear he was, slept on the giant white iceberg in the kitchen. The girls stayed with me.

When Mom returned to Buffalo, another guest arrived for an extended visit. This guest was four-legged and furry and marmalade-striped: my dear old gentleman cat, Sam, was back for a two-month stay while his constantly traveling owner was in Europe. It had been almost a year since our then seventeen-year-old patient had been diagnosed. His chronic leukemia was in remission, but he still needed daily medication. He had never stayed with me for longer than two weeks, and I was a little apprehensive about the length of this visit.

Sam hissed at my cats for a few hours when he arrived, but once he established himself on the windowsill with the rich green plants, he seemed to feel more comfortable. The plants thrived between his visits. He began pruning them.

His owner called weekly to check on Sam's progress. He was eating well, and the blood sample that I had taken to the hospital confirmed that he was still in remission. Daphne shadowed Sam, lurking behind the curtain when he ate on the windowsill. I fed him four times a day, and she knew that he always left a morsel or two on the plate. She allowed him to finish, and only when he jumped down from his perch would she move into his territory. Sam slept most of the day, and my other cats continued their daily routines, uninterrupted by his presence.

Four weeks into his visit Sam stopped eating. A change in daily habits is always cause for attention, but in a seventeen-and-a-half-year-old cat it is cause for alarm.

Sam was not vomiting, so I force-fed him baby food and chicken broth. He had severe diarrhea, and it was difficult for him to drink enough water on his own to maintain his hydration. This could affect his kidneys. For nine days I force-fed him, treated him with antibiotics, and gave him fluids under the skin. He seemed to be improving and only resented the subcutaneous fluids. He enjoyed the broth and baby food. Finally, toward the end of the second week, he appeared in the kitchen when I was feeding the rest of the family. He ate on his own.

He recovered rapidly once he began eating. We returned to normal. The episode brought us closer, and Sam now asked for more of my time. It was no longer medical attention that he sought, but affection. Our relationship changed, and he became more than a guest. Sam had a tremendous will to live. I had respected him before; now I loved him.

At the end of April Sam went home. No one seemed to miss him at the apartment. No one but me.

The spring semester was nearing an end, and I was anxious to complete my courses. As the days grew warmer and longer I found it more difficult to sit through lectures and to study.

Sometimes, those late spring afternoons when I came home

from work, and especially in May when I returned from school, I'd buy a bunch of lilacs on my way home. I'd set them in a vase in the front room and settle in my chair, listening to music. Slowly, as the fragrance drifted through the room, I'd close my eyes, returning to a memory that was not even mine. He bought her lilacs. He filled the rooms with them. Mom came home from work and walked into a garden of flowers, lavender and white, the fragrance filling every room. This plot of memory, buried in my mother's past, now grows within my life.

Natasha recalled me, as if to say it's another time. We are here now. We are your present. I stroked her chest and tummy where her fur had grown, covering the evidence of surgery. I thought of nothing but her.

When I first moved to New York, I was tense with the excitement of living in the big city. I lived in different neighborhoods, living with roommates and subletting apartments. When I finally got my own apartment, I chose the neighborhood in which I still live. Home, school, and work are all within walking distance. I can stroll along the streets, stopping to chat with storekeepers, waving at familiar faces. I know which ground-floor apartments house cats, and I visit the local establishments that keep them.

The big city has become for me a city full of little neighborhoods like mine. I may be one of the few tenants in New York who thinks her landlord is wonderful. He knows that I have cats. He considers this a weakness, even a fault, but he accepts us.

The Sunday after my last exam I was walking by the local grocery store when the manager ran out into the street.

"We've been looking for you," he said, pulling me out of the pedestrian traffic. "We need your help."

One of their chain stores located six blocks away had closed. The buildings on the entire block were being demolished the next morning. They had cleared the store of merchandise and equipment. For the past five days movers were in and out. Walls had been knocked down with pounding hammers and buzzing saws. Stranded in all this chaos was the store cat. He was now so frightened that he would allow only the store manager to feed him. He could pet him, but the cat panicked if he was handled. Tomorrow the building would be torn down. Our mission: rescue the cat.

I walked into the store and saw a thousand places for a cat to hide. There was one room with a door. We shut the windows in that room, despite the heat, the flies, and the smell. I had a blanket, a rope, a leash, and a carrier. Standing behind the door I waited for the other members of the team to direct the cat into the room. I waited an hour.

When the cat appeared, I shut the door, knowing how trapped he must feel. I followed him for another half-hour until I succeeded in slipping the rope around his neck. He pulled and twisted, fighting the trap, biting at the rope. I talked to him softly, trying to let him know that I wouldn't harm him. His fear made me tremble. I wanted to hug him, to pet him, to calm him, but he was fighting to escape what he thought was the enemy. I had no alternative. I could not leave him there to be buried by a crumbling building.

The manager came in, and I asked him for the blanket. Wrapping the cat, I attached the leash to his collar. The manager opened the carrier and I lifted the cat, loosening the rope as he landed in the box. The rope removed, we closed the lid.

The cat was moved to my local store, and I went home to clean my clothes and self, both thick with dust and dirt. My hands were still shaking from the ordeal. I imagine the cat was too.

In early June we admitted a pretty calico cat to the ward. She was dehydrated, not eating, and had a fever. Audrey suspected an infected uterus and confirmed her diagnosis with X rays and blood tests. While the cat was receiving fluids and antibiotics Audrey called her owner for permission to schedule surgery. This was a new client, and he informed Audrey that he wanted to think about the surgery.

We were both annoyed by the client's attitude. There was really nothing to think about. This cat did not have cancer. She had an illness that could be treated and cured by surgical removal of her uterus. She was nine years old, and there was every chance that she could live at least another nine years. The owner called back and instructed us to euthanize the cat. He would not consider any other alternative. Legally she was his cat, and the decision was his.

I carried the body down to our morgue. After nine years with this gentle cat, how could the owner betray her like this? I couldn't understand the small value that he had placed on her life.

Returning to the eighth floor, I got off the elevator and saw my old friend Stripes sitting in his carrier. Mrs. Firpo waved me over, and I saw that she had been crying.

"Sam, look at him. Just all of a sudden, yesterday, he got all bloated, just like my other cat. I'm so afraid he's got FIP."

Mrs. Firpo had already lost several cats to the feline-leuke-mia-virus-related diseases and to FIP. Feline infectious peritonitis is one of the most devastating diseases we see in cats. In one form of the disease protein-rich fluid accumulates in the body cavities, in the chest or, more commonly, the abdomen. The cats lose weight; they start to look haunted. They almost always die.

I touched her hand as her name was called. "I'll come in in a few minutes."

As I entered the room Audrey was telling her what Mrs. Firpo had already anticipated.

"I think it's FIP, but we'll take a sample of the fluid to send to the lab for confirmation."

"And if that's what it is," she interrupted, "then what?"

"Well, I can't be optimistic. After all, you've experienced this disease in your other cats. But let's make sure first that that's what we're dealing with. Is he still eating?"

"A little, but nothing like his old appetite. I can bring some food for him."

"Oh, that's okay," I said, "we have quite a variety."

"Well, maybe I'll make some chicken for him."

"Yes, that's different. I don't cook—we're totally catered here."

She smiled, and Audrey and I prepared the paperwork to admit him to the hospital.

"Can I come visit him?" she asked.

"Of course," I replied. "But first we'll make sure we know what he has and how long he'll have to stay."

I carried Stripes into the ward. He had overcome one fatal disease already. What were the chances of him surviving this second illness? Intellectually we knew that we were doing everything possible, but that knowledge offered little solace in the face of the overwhelming likelihood that he would die. Mrs. Firpo had other cats; Stripes was not even mine, but he was special to both of us.

Audrey came into the ward as I was feeding Stripes.

"How's he doing?" she asked. She had prescribed medication to decrease the fluid in his abdomen. Since he wasn't eating or drinking normally, he was also receiving fluids intravenously.

"He wants attention, and he seems interested in food, but he's not eating well. Where do we go from here?"

"Well, I've been thinking about that. We could try the conventional therapy."

"Even though our results have been poor," I said, completing her thought. But there was an alternative in her voice. "Or?" I encouraged.

"Or what do you think of trying a different drug? I'd like to try something new and send him home."

"We really have nothing to lose, do we?"

"No, the odds are against him, again. Let's give it a try."

We treated him. Mrs. Firpo came to pick him up that night. She was aware of the poor prognosis, but she was not ready to give up. If she had decided on euthanasia, based on her experience and ours, she would not have been wrong. But she was eager to have him home again, even though he looked about the same as when she had brought him in.

As I look out my window sometimes, memory drifts by on a cloud, pulling my attention with her as she slides across the sky. I see a fat white-and-tiger-striped cat rubbing against my father as he putters in the kitchen. Cans of wasted food lie on the sink, and Mitchie will not eat his cat food because Dad says that Mitchie says it's his day for chicken livers. And this too is real, though memory protects its images and presents them as a cornucopia of those best aspects. I hear Mitchie purring, and then my hand touches the softness of a cat, and I am startled to discover Evelyn purring loudly on my lap.

"Is Evelyn pregnant?" Mrs. Firpo asked on her next visit to the clinic, watching her sway across the room.

"No, she's just lost her girlish figure," I explained. "I've been hearing wonderful reports on his progress," I said, looking down at Stripes. He had been home for one week.

"I think the fluid is gone, and his appetite is better than ever," she replied. "I can't believe the change in him. He's following me around, demanding food again."

I smiled, thinking of the habits that absence promotes. This normality is what we strive for, along with a clinical improvement. But it is the attitude, in Stripes the attitude toward food, that indicates to us that he is improving. When a sick animal begins to show joy in his old ways, to sit in the bathtub again, to play once more with his rabbit's foot, to scratch on the bark of a plant, it is as though he had been gone a short time, and now is home again. Afraid to ask how long, lest asking should prompt a departure, we accept the present in silence.

We were amazed, pleased, and respectful of Stripes's miraculous recovery. His fluid had disappeared and he was hungry and arrogant again. We didn't know how long this improvement would last; he could relapse at any time. We decided to recheck him weekly and to continue treatment.

I picked up the summer school catalogue from Hunter, looking for another biology course for the six-week term. The only offerings from that department were courses that I had already completed. I turned the pages of the catalogue from biology to English and saw that a course in the writings of Virginia Woolf was being offered. I registered.

I don't know if I had intentionally ignored my love for literature, or if I had hidden it so safely in the past that I had

142

forgotten it. I had turned to science when literature no longer seemed relevant in my new work. English had seemed to isolate me when I needed to be involved. I needed to be an integral part of the unit, and I had associated the fulfillment of that need with a degree in the sciences. But suddenly another need emerged. The need itself had been present all along, I suppose, and only my rediscovery of it was sudden. I remembered the balance that I had sought in my life, seeing now that I had pursued both extremes separately. I needed to discover for myself how I felt about my life and the other lives so intricately interwoven with mine.

I didn't want to commit myself to a plan that would structure and control my life, dominating every aspect of it. Instead I wanted to develop my knowledge in specific areas so that I could better understand my work. But I wanted more than work in my life. I wanted and needed the excitement of literature. I had felt isolated before; now I felt that literature offered me the freedom and opportunity to touch other lives in different ways.

I savored the hours of reading. Classes met four nights a week for two hours, and I felt sinfully immersed in literature. At the completion of the course I was unwilling to stop. I was anxious to read and especially to reread my collection of books. I wanted to see if I read differently now, if my perceptions had changed. I decided to take the fall semester off to indulge my literary needs and to sort out my feelings about the future.

Our Labor Day weekend clinic was lightly booked. Most of our clients had arranged to come in the previous Thursday or the following Tuesday so that they could go away for the three-day holiday.

I recognized Monica's friend, Margaret, in the waiting room with Mykonos.

"Is Monica all right?" I asked. I was alarmed, because Monica had mentioned the last time she was in how ill the chemotherapy made her. Looking at Mykonos, Monica had smiled and said softly, "But look how well he's doing now."

Monica was hospitalized for sepsis associated with her treatments. The drugs had indiscriminately killed both cancer and normal cells, including her infection-fighting cells.

"She's really angry with her doctor," Margaret related. "Her first words when she was out of isolation were, 'That bastard almost killed me!' He refused to see her when she complained of illness. He felt that that was a normal reaction."

"How is she recovering?" I asked.

"She's a fighter, as you know. She seems to be improving."

"Will she be coming home soon?"

"Yes, I think so. She misses her cats."

The Smiths brought Oliver in on the Saturday of Labor Day weekend. The disease had spread to his central nervous system. He walked slowly and with difficulty. He had spent the entire summer in Maine, receiving treatment from a local veterinarian.

"He had such a wonderful summer," Mrs. Smith told us. "We walked along the beach, and sometimes he left me to play with his seagull. But at night he sat with me on the porch, listening and rocking."

"Not many cats have their own personal seagull." I smiled.

"But it is," she insisted, thinking I doubted it. "He comes every year, and they chase each other back and forth. Then Oliver gets tired and walks out to his rock to sun himself. He gets so upset when the tide comes in and he can't get back to the beach!"

We laughed in memory of this Oliver who perhaps had stayed in Maine. For the handsome striped tiger on the table the days began to seem too long. It was not easy to let go of this life that had shared so much joy with all of us. He had given us almost five years of happiness. We had treated his disease for almost two years. But Oliver's joy was in the past. The present brought with it only pain.

I held him as I had held Clancy, years before, watching the tiger stripes blur through my tears. We cried, all of us, for Oliver, for Clancy, and for the seagull in Maine who had lost his summer friend. Summer was over.

Chapter 16

Clinic was ending as the phone rang. It had been a busy and satisfying day.

An unfamiliar voice spoke my name.

"Yes, this is Samantha," I replied.

"I'm Margaret Hooper, Monica's friend."

"Oh yes, of course," I responded. "Is there a problem with one of the cats?"

"No, no, it's not that. I'm calling about Monica, to tell you that she died about an hour ago."

I heard Margaret on the phone, telling me what had happened. Monica had developed pneumonia in her immuno-suppressed state. Although she seemed to be improving, she had arrested on Friday, and she died just this morning.

"What can we do to help?" I asked after a long pause.

"Well, I'm waiting now for her family to arrive, and then

we'll go to her apartment. I suppose we'll have to put the cats to sleep."

"Oh, no," I interrupted, "the cats were so important to Monica. Please, let us take them. After all, we gave her Sadie."

"Yes, that's true. And she did fight so hard to keep Mykonos alive."

"I think we owe her that. We'll take them."

We agreed to talk again the next day, and in the meantime she would feed them as planned.

Mrs. Smith had also called and left a message for me. Several weeks had passed since Oliver's death.

"Hi, Mrs. Smith, it's Samantha. I understand you called."

"Yes, dear, I wanted to ask you if you'd like to stay at our place in Maine. I was there last week, and it's still lovely weather. I know how much you love it up there."

"Your timing is perfect," I replied. "I was just thinking how nice it would be to get away for a few days. Would it really be all right?"

"Of course. I meant to offer last time, but we were all so upset. You know, I looked for Oliver's seagull this time, to tell him, but he wasn't there. Isn't that strange?"

"Well, I wonder if he doesn't know already."

"Do you suppose he does?" she asked, believing it herself.

"Yes, yes, I suppose he does."

In a few days I called Margaret. She was staying at Monica's apartment, helping the family sort through Monica's belongings.

"How are you feeling?" I asked.

"Well, there's been so much to do that I haven't really had much time to think," she replied.

"Have you had any time to yourself?"

"Yes, I spent some time alone, and then with some of our friends. We cried together, remembering things."

"And how are the cats?"

"You know, it's so strange—Mykonos and I never really liked one another too much. I don't think he forgave me for advising Monica to euthanize him when he was so sick. But when I came here from the hospital the Saturday after she died, he came over to me on the couch. He kept meowing and pushing his face against me. I really think he knew."

"He was very close to Monica. How do they seem now? Are they both eating?"

"Yes, they seem to be fine as long as someone is here in the apartment. I'll be staying another week or ten days, and then I think I'll take my vacation."

"Yes, I imagine you're exhausted. Do you want us to take them now?"

"No, I think they're comfortable here. I mean, they're used to the apartment, and as long as I'll be here they won't be lonely."

"Well, that will work out perfectly. I was thinking of taking some time off now, but I'll be back when you're ready to leave. I'll take them then."

She was a good friend, and we both felt that Monica would have been relieved about the cats and their future.

I asked Linda if she could feed my cats while I went to Maine. She was glad to.

"Things seem under control at the moment," I told her. "Natasha's due for her treatment this weekend, so I'll give it. She should be fine while I'm gone. One more thing. Don't throw out the Q-Tips on the floor. Sam carries them around, and he wants them where he puts them."

"Are you taking anyone with you?" she asked.

"No, it's a long bus ride," I replied. "This time I think I'll go alone."

It was as though the sun had finally emerged from a sky crowded with clouds. Knowing that other clouds awaited, I wanted to see, in the intensity of daylight, beyond the tall buildings that hindered my vision. I wanted time with my memories, time to touch again the feelings that more immediate needs had overshadowed. Going alone? Oh, no. No, I was taking with me all the names and faces, all the stories, the incidents that had shaped my life.

Life insists, in each form it takes, that the line must be drawn at one's endurance. One must say, to protect all that pervades the inner chambers, here is the line. This is the limit: I cannot step beyond.

My days had been full of challenges and rewards. Some of the cats I had met when I first started working in oncology had become memories, but each was a memory lovingly recalled when I met a new patient. Some of those first cats were still alive and doing well. I had learned a great deal from our patients in these years. I had discovered the individuality of each cat in personal terms and in terms of disease and response to therapy. I had learned the importance of a quality life, and the sorrowful dignity of death. We were still learning in the unit, and our patients were benefiting from our growth and experience.

I had not gone away since Fledermaus died. On those days that seemed to drag me down with sorrow I would think that I had reached my limit. And then, walking slowly across the waiting room I would see the nervous gestures of a woman waiting with her cat. It was her first time here, and for her this feline in the carrier, this cat we had not met, was the prettiest, the cleverest, the best cat in the world. And I'd know that she was right. He was not yet a part of my life until I stopped and smiled and asked, "What's his name?"

I had lived intensely and emotionally with our patients, and now I was full. I needed to sort out my memories, put them in order, and make room for new ones. And so, on a night in early October I boarded the bus that would take me to Oliver Cromwell's home in Maine.

Sitting on the porch overlooking the bay, I thought of Mrs. Smith, and how she and Oliver watched and listened here as the earth sighed. Looking out toward the ocean nothing interrupted the approach of wave upon wave. One by one they climbed toward me, each separate, each distinct. Now merging, now one, and still they kept coming.

I thought of Monica, and how we sat in the waiting room as she selected the ornaments for Sadie and Mykonos to place on our Christmas tree. I thought of her apartment and of the lovely objects that she had acquired throughout the years. Each meant something special to her no doubt, each recalling a time, a place, a person. But they were only things. Monica valued life, the miracle of each tomorrow. Sadie and Mykonos were what remained of her. Much of her life had been devoted to their comfort. Many decisions in her lifetime had revolved around their well-being. Now only the memory of this gentle woman remained. Memory and Sadie and Mykonos. They were her finest living memory.

Do we all leave behind these lives of shared love? These days, such days of sharing quality, quality that is learned and passed on to others. Monica's quality, Dad's, Clancy's, the Maus's. All of us participating for a time, and the earth going on when we stop. Is it changed for our having been here? Is it different, is it better? Or is it we who change?

The waves, the wind, my past, this present—this moment of confusion, the blurring of lines, of boundaries that separate my life from others—leading now to a moment, no longer unsettled, but quiet with peace. Here, on the edge of the world, here, on the brink of eternity, here, for a moment, it is enough.

The seagulls are honking in the distance as I follow a single gull who rides the waves I love as they sneak up the rocky beach. I know it is not Oliver Cromwell's friend. He is not here, and there his rock sits shining in the sun. I will never see it caressed away by waves, the waves I cannot change. He is not here. So many friends have gone. They mark the years that pass, and give the days their quality.

I discover her anew in each black cat I see. She is present in my joys and deepest sorrows, and reflected in the eyes of one who loves his cat. And sometimes, when a grayness falls upon an autumn day, or when the air is full of promises of rain, sometimes then I feel her near. In this moment, memory and senses in accord, reminiscences blend, and time has no meaning. The wind lingers in my presence, inviting me to share a secret, somewhere out of time. This young precocious breeze, just a whisper when we met before, has grown into a sturdy winter wind. She is with me, as real as the winter snow that blends the tears upon my face. And it is only when I try to touch her, to make her linger yet awhile, that she dies all over again. A snowflake in my hand, she is like a fragment of melody that I find myself humming unawares. Evasive and elusive, a song without words, a song with no end.

While somewhere else as I now say good-bye again, as shadows of my shadow pass before me, somewhere else a cat leaps to the windowsill to greet the morning sun. The black cat stretches beyond her length and purrs, harmonic with the world.